This book focuses on the exciting revival of Crewel and Silk Ribbon embroidery and depicts in full colour the work of the author, her students and top teachers. Comprehensive step by step instructions, accompanied by clear line drawings and water colours, take the reader through a host of innovative embroidery techniques combined with ribbon and paint work. A *Portfolio of Sketches and Stitches* at the end of the book will be a needlewoman's constant reference for many years to come. *Just Flowers* will prove to be an invaluable and enchanting source of inspiration for both the beginner and the experienced floral artist.

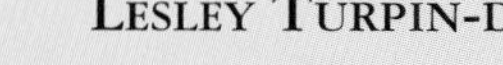

LESLEY TURPIN-DELPORT

Published by TRIPLE T Publishing cc
Cape Town

Front cover: Terracotta terrace – Colenso Road (Lesley Turpin-Delport and Lesley Lewis)

Back cover: A potted corner (Beryl Soller)

Monogram on page 5: Eleanor Jubiler

First Published 1994
Second impression March 1995

TRIPLE T Publishing cc
29 Colenso Road
Claremont 7700
Cape Town South Africa

NORTH AMERICAN DISTRIBUTOR
Quilters Resources inc.
P.O. Box 148850
Chicago IL 60614

Other books published by Triple T Publishing
SATIN & SILK RIBBON EMBROIDERY by Lesley Turpin Delport ISBN 0-620-17755-1
TWO CUSHIONS AND A QUILT by Sue Akerman ISBN 0-958-38731-1

Typesetting: Mandy Moss
Reproduction: Hirt and Carter (Pty) Ltd, Cape Town
Printed by Creda Press, Cape Town

Text, illustrations and photography: Lesley Turpin-Delport
Calligraphy: Anne Marie Moore
Special paint techniques by Philip Preston Delport

ISBN 0958-3873-3-8 (Hard cover edition)
0958-3873-2-X (Soft cover edition)

Contents

Authors Acknowledgements

My special thanks to all who have contributed to this book and to my family and friends who have shown so much patience and understanding during the production.

Sue Akerman
Renske Biddulph
Gay Booysen
Sandra Caister
Denise Crain
Linda de Luca
Nicola Delport
Nanda Dos Santos
Rachelle Druian
Ann Foulner
Sharon Frittelli
Margot Gawith
Felicity Goldstein
Sheila Hill
Paulette Hodes
Carmen Isaacs
Eleanor Jubiler
Val Lane
Julie Lazarus
Lesley Lewis
Anne Neill
Tracy Neill
Geoffrey Preston-Thomas
Bridget Price
Lynn Reid
Leone Segal
Susan Sittig
Gillian Smith
Beryl Soller
Di Thompson
Mike Tripp
Avril Walsh
Ethel Walt
Madge Wulfsohn

AND MY SINCERE GRATITUDE TO THE SAMMY MARKS MUSEUM, PRETORIA

THE EMBROIDERY THREADS USED FOR MOST ITEMS IN THIS BOOK WERE SUPPLIED BY D. M. C. (SOUTH AFRICA)

Introduction

It is ten years since I first put pen to paper to share my love of creative threads with all needlecrafters. My initial training as a Fine Arts student has allowed a freedom of spirit when an embroidery idea comes to mind. I enjoy experimenting with crewel stitches and different yarns. The common denominator over the last years has been a constant passion for flowers in threads. I can now share my inspiration with you through the pages of 'Just Flowers'.

Let's take a journey of discovery, learning a floral vocabulary in crewel and silk ribbon embroidery.

The silk ribbon flows through the Floral ABC with a "how to" in the *Portfolio of Stitches and Sketches*. It is fun and quick to do and so tactile. Much finer, but equally special are the sweet sixteen spring and summer flowers in crewel stitches and a miniature herb collection.

Once you have this knowledge of flowers at your fingertips, move on to the idea of underpainting for a different dimension. You will notice that at times, I guide you step-by-step but with other designs, I provide a gentle watercolour for you to enjoy and use in your own special way.

There are many different ideas for you to share and if you create just one tiny flower of your own, in fine thread, then our floral adventure together will have been worth every stitch.

Do get creative!!

A Story o

The Samuel Marks Museum story

The Samuel Marks Museum, situated on the outskirts of Pretoria, South Africa was Sammy's beautiful home Zwartkoppies Hall. Sammy was a renowned and respected South African pioneer.

It was to Zwartkoppies Hall that Sammy brought his very young bride Bertha Guttman whom he married in Sheffield, England in 1884. Apart from the cost of erecting the home and bringing the furniture, silver, glass, crockery, cutlery and linen from England, imagine the problems in organising the whole project and arranging for the transport by ox-wagon of the materials. Imagine too the young bride's feelings finding herself in a strange country, among strange folk and with the nearest town, Pretoria, about 23 km away.

One hundred years later, on a hazy autumn morning I was giving a silk ribbon embroidery class, under the

Sammy Marks – His daughter, Girlie.

Detail bow and forget-me-nots

Detail ribbon dais

mbroidery

›ines on the lawns of this gracious home. While we vere enjoying a break of cucumber sandwiches and ıerbal tea, the curator of the museum, who had shown ;reat interest in what we were doing, excitedly .nnounced that, hanging in the sitting room, were wo portraits with mounts embellished in silk ribbon.)ur entire class rushed into the magnificent house, .nd there to our sheer delight we discovered the ›eautiful works pictured here. The portraits are of ›ammy's daughters Dolly and Girlie and the silk work s in perfect condition other than a slight fading of the ›ackground silk. The embroidery must have been done n *circa* 1900, and ninety four years later, we were able o enjoy the rediscovery of these charming pieces. Vith renewed energy and enthusiasm the embroidery ›arty returned to their silk ribbon posies with the ›irdsong around us echoing our thrill of the day's liscovery.

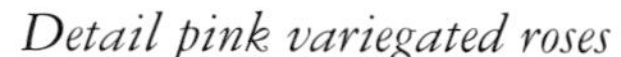

Detail pink variegated roses

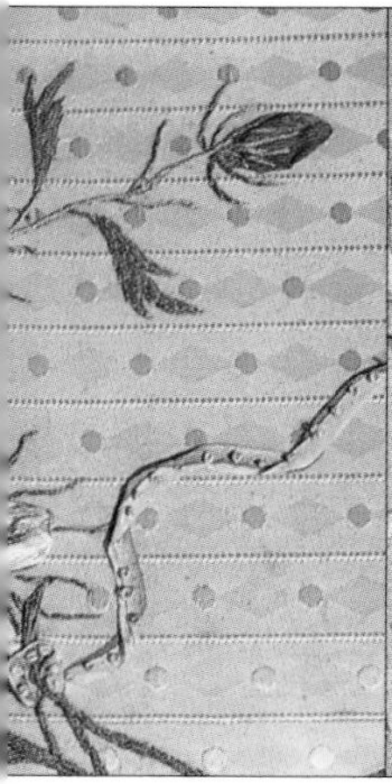

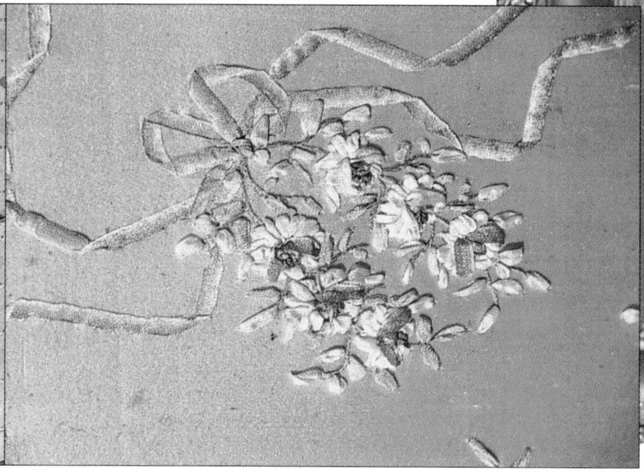

Sammy Marks – His daughter, Dolly

The Embroidery Basket

Arranged in a pretty whicker basket, embroidery notions are always at hand when you feel like a little fancy work. Selecting exciting fabric and choosing the right needle and thread to match are part of the little pleasures of life that give so much enjoyment.
Embroidery is a creative process. Free your imagination and experiment with different threads and express your creativity.

THE EMBROIDERY BASKET
A collection of miniatures shows the importance of the embroidery basket for the avid needle crafter even in a doll's house world.

Threads

Stranded Cotton (Floss)

A shiny six strand thread which can be split into 1, 2, to 6 threads according to the thickness of the fabric, the desired effect and the embroiderers special know-how. It is the best choice for cross stitch, padded and unpadded satin stitch and crewel embroidery. In 8m skeins, 397 colours.

My favourite colours for the flowers are the following:

Pinks –	DMC	221, 223, 224, and 225
Lilacs –	DMC	3041, 3042
Blues –	DMC	930, 932, 3750, 3752 and 3753
Yellows –	DMC	744, 745 and 3046
Greens –	DMC	500, 501, 502, 503 and 372
Apricots –	DMC	3778, 3779

Perle Cotton

Shiny, twisted thread, ideal for beginners: it does not come untwisted and thus ensures uniform stitches. Excellent results on medim, coarse linen and aida fabrics. Available in skeins or balls. Three thread sizes, Nos 3,5 and 8, and more than 250 colours.

Soft Cotton

(Tapestry cotton)
Thick, matt thread, 100% cotton is very easy to use on coarse or basket-weave canvases. Soft and flexible.
In 10m skeins, 285 colours.

CHOOSING YOUR SILK RIBBON.
There is a wonderful selection of silk ribbons available. Glorious colours have been matched against the painting for the final embroidery design.

Coton A Broder/ Flower Thread
Fine, matt cotton thread.

Tapestry Wool
Suitable for embroidery on softly textured, loosely woven material.

Crewel Wool
Mothproof, 100% pure virgin wool, soft and fine, ideal for delicate wool work.

Pure Silk, rayon, viscose, linen and metallic thread
These are a number of other thread types which are exciting when mixed together to create different textures and colour combinations. Some craft shops have hand-dyed, variegated threads which are marvellous for free style embroidery.

Quilting threads
Commercial quilting threads are now available in all colours, but if you can't find any, use a pure cotton thread (No 30) and run it through beeswax to prevent it tangling.

RIBBONS
(Pure silk, raw silk and satin ribbon)
Pure silk ribbon is available in 2mm, 3.5mm, 7mm and 13mm. It is so soft that it can be pulled through the background fabric just like embroidery floss. Rayon ribbon works well using the silk ribbon techniques. Raw silk webbing (see Delightful Daisies) can be manipulated onto the background fabric and pulled through, if the fabric is not too fine. Satin ribbon is best manipulated off the background fabric. Construct leaves and flowers as free-form shapes and then work them onto the background using invisible stitches.

EMBROIDERY SCISSORS
Light with fine, pointed ends to cut thread cleanly.

THIMBLE
A must for embroidery comfort.

Embroidery Fabrics

All fabrics can be used for embroidery.

Embroidery fabrics which are highly recommended:

- fine and medium fabrics; pure linen, pure cotton, linen cotton mixture
- more open fabrics to make counting threads and stitches easier, such as coarse linen and even-weave.
- Exotic fabrics such as moiré taffetta, pure silk, raw silk, velvet and fine corduroy and antique handkerchiefs.

Embroidery Frame

The cloth, stretched on the frame, does not pucker. Various frames are available. They can be held in the hand, fixed to a stand or to the edge of a table. They come in several diameters.

Needles

- Use crewel (embroidery) needles for fine embroidery. Sharp tip, small eye.
- Chenille needles for candlewicking and silk ribbon embroidery. Sharp tip, long eye.
- Tapestry needles for woollen embroidery. Blunt tip, long eye.
- Straw (or sharps) needles for specialist stitches such as bullion and cast-on buttonhole. Very small eye, long shaft.
- Betweens for quilting. Small eye, very short shaft.
- Bead needles for beading. Small eye, long and very thin shaft.

Beads

A selection of tiny seed beads, pearls and bugle beads is very handy to work into your embroidery for shine and dimension.

Permanent Markers

A permanent black fine-liner is used in the mixed media designs. Always test your pen to see that it is in fact colour fast. Different nib widths are available for fine or coarse work. Ink in your outline before you begin the paintwork.

Fabric Paints

A water based, permanent paint is ideal.

Try different size paint brushes: a fat stiff bristle brush will give a good stipple or drag effect; a medium size, stiff bristle brush is good for the smaller areas and a small fine brush is needed for delicate detail.

Begin by testing your paint on a small piece of scrap fabric to gain a little confidence. Use the paint, very diluted, to give the delicate water colour effect. Dry paint will give a good stipple and a creamy consistency is best for filling in. Heat seal the paintwork by ironing with a hot iron.The black outline can be worked into with a permanent fine marker if you have painted too darkly.

A POTTED CORNER

Fabric paint and hand applique give extra dimension to an embroidered corner of terracotta pots. (Beryl Soller)

A Floral A B C

Enjoy an A to Z of silk ribbon flowers. The silk ribbon is 3.5 and 7mm wide and each stitch is illustrated through the alphabet. The crewel stitches are in DMC floss in two strands, unless otherwise stated. *(see Portfolio of Stitches and Sketches)*

CAMELOT Learn the A to Z of silk ribbon flowers and then create a garland of your favourite flowers – ideal for 'happy ever-aftering' as in the days of Camelot. *(Di Thompson)*

THE ABC STORY

The letters A to Z are in bottle green silk ribbon (No. 75).
Lay the ribbon down with stab stitch on the straight strokes and split stitch on the curves. The 'leaf-like' tips are in inverted stab stitch Stabilise the letters with colonial knots in bottle green floss (DMC 500) in two strands.
(See page 80–81 for details)

ARUM LILY

Blooms	Inverted stab stitch	white 7mm silk ribbon and bullion knot centre, yellow floss (DMC 745
Stems	Stem stitch	green floss (DMC 502)
Leaves	Inverted stab stitch	green 7mm silk ribbon (No.32)

BLEEDING HEART

Blooms	Inverted stab stitch	red silk ribbon (No. 93) and green silk ribbon (No. 32)
Stamens	Extended french knot	yellow floss (DMC 745)
Stems	Stem stitch	green floss (DMC 502)
Leaves	Fly stitch	green silk ribbon (No. 32)

CORNFLOWERS

Blooms	Inverted stab stitch	pink (No. 158), blue silk (No. 126), and white silk ribbons
	Colonial knot centre	yellow floss (DMC 745)
Stems	Stem stitch	green floss (DMC 502)
Leaves	Inverted stab stitch	green silk ribbon (No. 33)

DAFFODIL

Blooms	Inverted stab stitch	yellow silk ribbon (No. 14)
	Buttonhole	yellow floss (DMC 744)
Stems	Stem stitch	green floss (DMC 502)
Leaves	Chain	green floss (DMC 502)

ERICA

Blooms	Stab stitch	lilac silk ribbon (No. 178)
	Colonial knot	bright pink silk ribbon (No. 128)
Stems	Stem stitch	green floss (DMC 501) and light green floss (DMC 504)
Leaves	Stab stitch	green silk ribbon (No. 33)

FUCHSIA

Blooms	Stab stitch	light and rose pink silk ribbon (Nos. 157 and 158)
	and lazy daisy	burgundy floss (DMC 221) 1 strand
Stems	Stem stitch	bright green floss (DMC 369)
Leaves	Stab stitch	light green silk ribbon (No. 31)
Stamens	Extended french knots	yellow floss (DMC 745)

GERANIUM

Blooms	Stab stitch	red silk ribbon (No. 93)
Stems	Stem stitch	green floss (DMC 501)
Leaves	Stab stitch	green silk ribbon (No. 33)

HYDRANGEA

Blooms	Colonial knots	pink and blue and lilac silk ribbons (Nos. 158, 126 and 178)
Leaves	Inverted stab stitch	green 7mm wide silk ribbon (No. 32

IRIS

Blooms	Iris stitch	lilac and plum silk ribbon (Nos. 178 and 177)
Stems	Stem stitch	green floss (DMC 501)
Leaves	Inverted stab stitch	green silk ribbon (No. 33)

A to M of silk ribbon flowers *(Ann Foulner)*

N to Z of silk ribbon flowers *(Ann Foulner)*

JASMINE

Blooms	Stab stitch	light pink and burgundy silk ribbon (Nos. 157 and 159)
	lazy daisy	burgundy floss (DMC 221) 1 strand)
Stems	Stem stitch	green floss (DMC 502)
Leaves	Inverted stab stitch	green silk ribbon (No. 32)
Calyx	Lazy daisy	green floss (DMC 502)

KINGFISHER DAISY

Blooms	Inverted stab stitch	blue silk ribbon (No. 126)
	Colonial knot centres	yellow floss (DMC 744)
Leaves	Colonial knot	green silk ribbon (No 33)

LAVENDER

Blooms	Mock bullion	lilac silk ribbon (No. 179)
Stems and Leaves	Feather stitch	light and dark green floss – 1 strand of each (DMC 504 and 501)

MARIGOLD

Blooms	Fluted/ruched petals	yellow and orange silk ribbon (Nos. 14 and 168)
Stems	Stem stitch	green floss (DMC 502)
Leaves	Inverted stab stitch	green 7mm silk ribbon (No. 32)

NASTURTIUM

Blooms	Inverted stab stitch	yellow and apricot silk ribbon (Nos. 14 and 168)
Stems	Stem stitch	green floss (DMC 368)
Leaves	Buttonhole pinwheel	green floss (DMC 368)

OXALIS

Blooms	Stab stitch	pink silk ribbon (No 163)
Calyx	Stab stitch	green silk ribbon (No 33)
Stems	Stem stitch	green floss (DMC 502)
Leaves	Stab stitch	green silk ribbon (No 33)

PERIWINKLE

Blooms	Inverted stab stitch	blue silk ribbon (No. 44)
Stems	Stem stitch	green floss (DMC 501)
Leaves	Stab stitch	green silk ribbon (No 32)

QUINCE

Blooms	3D petal daisies	white silk ribbon
Stamens	Extended french knots	yellow and pink floss (DMC 745 and 224) 1 strand
Stems	Stem stitch	light green floss (DMC 369)
Leaves	Stab stitch	green silk ribbon (No 31)

ROSE

Blooms	Woven spider's web rose	pink silk ribbon (No. 158)
Buds	Colonial knot and lazy daisy	pink silk ribbon (No. 158)
Leaves	Inverted stab stitch	green silk ribbon (No 33)

SNOWDROP

Blooms	Inverted stab stitch	white silk ribbon
	Colonial knot	green floss (DMC 501) and
	Lazy daisy	green floss (DMC 502) in 1 strand
Calyx	Stab stitch	green silk ribbon (No 31)
Stems	Stem stitch	light green floss (DMC 503)
Leaves	Chain	green floss (DMC 502)

Tulips

Blooms	Inverted stab stitch	yellow silk ribbon (Nos. 12 and 14) tipped with fly stitch in burgundy floss (DMC 221)
Stems	Stem stitch	light green floss (DMC 369)
Leaves	Chain	light green floss (DMC 369) whipped on one side in DMC 502

Ursinia

Blooms	3D petal daisy	yellow silk ribbon (no. 14)
	Colonial knot centre	orange and mustard silk ribbon (Nos. 168 and 51)
Stems	Stem stitch	green floss (DMC 503)
Leaves	Stab stitch	green silk ribbon (No 33)

Violet

Blooms	Inverted stab stitch	violet silk ribbon (No 177)
	Colonial knot centre	yellow floss (DMC 745)
Stems	Stem stitch	green floss (DMC 502)
Leaves	Buttonhole	green floss (DMC 501)

Wisteria

Blooms	Colonial knots	light and dark lilac silk ribbon (Nos. 178 and 179)
Stems	Stem stitch	light green floss (DMC 368)
Leaves	Bullion and lazy daisy	green floss (DMC 368)

Xmas Pointsettia

Blooms	Bullion lazy daisy	red silk ribbon (No 93)
	bullion knot centre	yellow floss (DMC 744)

Yesterday, Today and Tomorrow

Blooms	Inverted stab stitch	white, lilac and blue silk ribbon (Nos. 178, 179 and 126)
Stems	Stem stitch	green floss (DMC 501)
Leaves	Stab stitch	green silk ribbon (No. 33)

Zinnia

Blooms	Fluted/ruched petals	burgundy and orange silk ribbon (Nos. 114 and 168)
Stems	Stem stitch	green floss (DMC 503)
Leaves	Inverted stab stitch	green silk ribbon (No. 32)

These silk ribbon flowers and techniques appear in the following chapters wherever silk ribbon is used.

FLORAL MONOGRAMS (Gay Booysen)

Imagine that you had picked your favourite flowers and arranged them in the outlines of your special initials

Sweet Sixteen Embroidery Sampler

Crewel stitches are combined to create sixteen delightful spring and summer flowers. Quilt the background of alternate blocks to give exciting texture to the design.

This embroidery sampler is an excellent way of learning a vocabulary of crewel stitches ideal for garden flowers. *(Sandra Caister)*

How to Make Up a Sampler

Materials

- Background fabric (40 x 40cm)
- Polyester wadding (40 x 40cm)
- Muslin (40 x 40cm)
- A selection of embroidery floss
- Quilting thread
- Crewel needle
- Between needle

Instructions

Position the cotton fabric over the design and lightly sketch the flowers and grid onto the background *(See page 82–85).* Use a light box or hold the fabric up against a window, if difficulty is experienced in tracing the design.

NOTE: If you wish to omit the quilted background, tack the muslin behind the ground fabric before you begin the embroidery. Wet and iron your muslin before placing it behind the prepared fabric. See that the warp and the weft of the muslin and the top cotton match (ie. the greatest stretch is in the same direction) and baste together. (The muslin gives body and a foundation for beginning and ending neatly).

Study the labelled sketch in the chapter, *Portfolio of Sketches and Stitches* as well as the photographs and enjoy creating the different flowers using the crewel stitch glossary provided.

Once all the flowers are complete, embroider the grid in whipped chain; the chain is in two strands of ecru floss, whipped in two strands of light green floss.

Textile Sandwich

To quilt the background of the design, ie. alternate blocks as shown in the photograph, prepare the "textile sandwich" as follows: Muslin, then the wadding and finally the ground fabric, right side up. Tack outwards from the centre towards each of the corners.

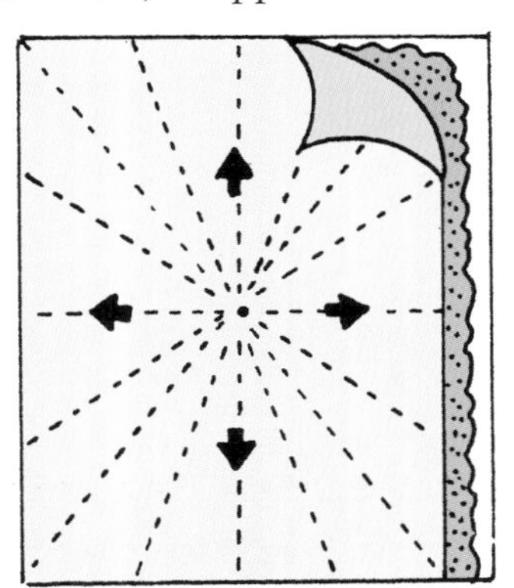

MICHAELMAS DAISY DETAIL

The well controlled bullion petals are complimented by the ripple of the background quilting.

Use a "between" needle and ecru quilting thread. The quilting stitch is a small running stitch moving in a vertical direction. Be sure to squeeze the layers together to give the quilt rhythm but do not pucker.
Once the design is complete, make the block up into a piped/frilled cushion or into a framed picture with interesting mount boards and a guilded frame
You now have a vocabulary of free-style crewel stitch flowers at your fingertips.

To make up a cushion cover.

Purchase piping or a border fabric for a delightful frill.(Double fullness is required) Run a gathering thread along the edge of the frill and pull up the gathers to fit the embroidered background. Attach the frill/piping to the square. Make sure that the corners are well gathered if you use a frill.
Cut two pieces of fabric 30 x 40cm for the backs of the cushion. Turn under 2.5cm along one long edge of each backing piece to form a hem.
Place the backing pieces right sides down over the embroidered top piece, positioning the hemmed edges in the centre.
Machine straight stitch around the cushion, trim and overlock the seams and turn through. Sew on tiny buttons and make hand sewn buttonholes. Purchase or make an inside cushion.

THE GARDEN AT WINDYBROW – *Here a selection of the "Sweet Sixteen" flowers have been grouped together in a spectacular garden corner.* (Ann Foulner)

The fine quilted blocks provide an interesting contrast to the plain blocks, creating a balance for the design. (Sandra Caișter)

Delightful Daisies

The daisy family is the largest family of flowers in the world. Their charm lies in the basic simplicity of the large disc-like centre and radiating petals.
The numbers of petals vary and the colours are different according to their group but the country charm always identifies the basic daisy. This chapter provides just a few interpretations of the multi-faceted daisy family.

Shasta Daisy Designs

Underpaint the daisy with white fabric paint petals and yellow centres. Mix your paint to a creamy consistency and apply the white to the bottle green background fabric, in sweeping strokes. Dot the centres with yellow paint and create soft, sweeping leaves in green paint. Work into some of the daisies with white silk ribbon in stab stitch and colonial knot the centre with yellow silk ribbon. The leaves can be overworked in fly stitch in two strands of green floss and the stems in whipped chain.
If you are not comfortable with the paint techniques use the design on page 25 in silk ribbon and floss.

Left: PATIO CUSHION *A vibrant design to adorn verdigris garden furniture, striking in white paint and silk ribbon.* (Lesley Turpin-Delport)

Below: INSPIRATION *The simplicity of the shasta daisy with snow white petals and bright yellow centres was the inspiration for the patio cushion.*

Below left: UNDERPAINTING *The bottle green background provides an exciting foil for the energetic white petals.*

Below middle: CUSHION DETAIL *Silk ribbon is worked into the paint in simple stab stitch to give a sheen and dimension to the painted daisies.*

NDIGENOUS DAISIES *A selection of indigenous daisies in crewel combinations based a painting by botanical artist Barbara Jeppe.* (Ann Foulner)

SUNSET SUNFLOWERS *A field of golden sunflowers in bullion knots on an underpainting of silk paint on pure silk fabric.* (Sue Akerman)

SUNFLOWERS *The word daisy comes from day's eye. The daisy plant must have sun. Here sunflowers bloom in silk ribbon stab stitch, with colonial knots and beaded centres.* (Di Thompson)

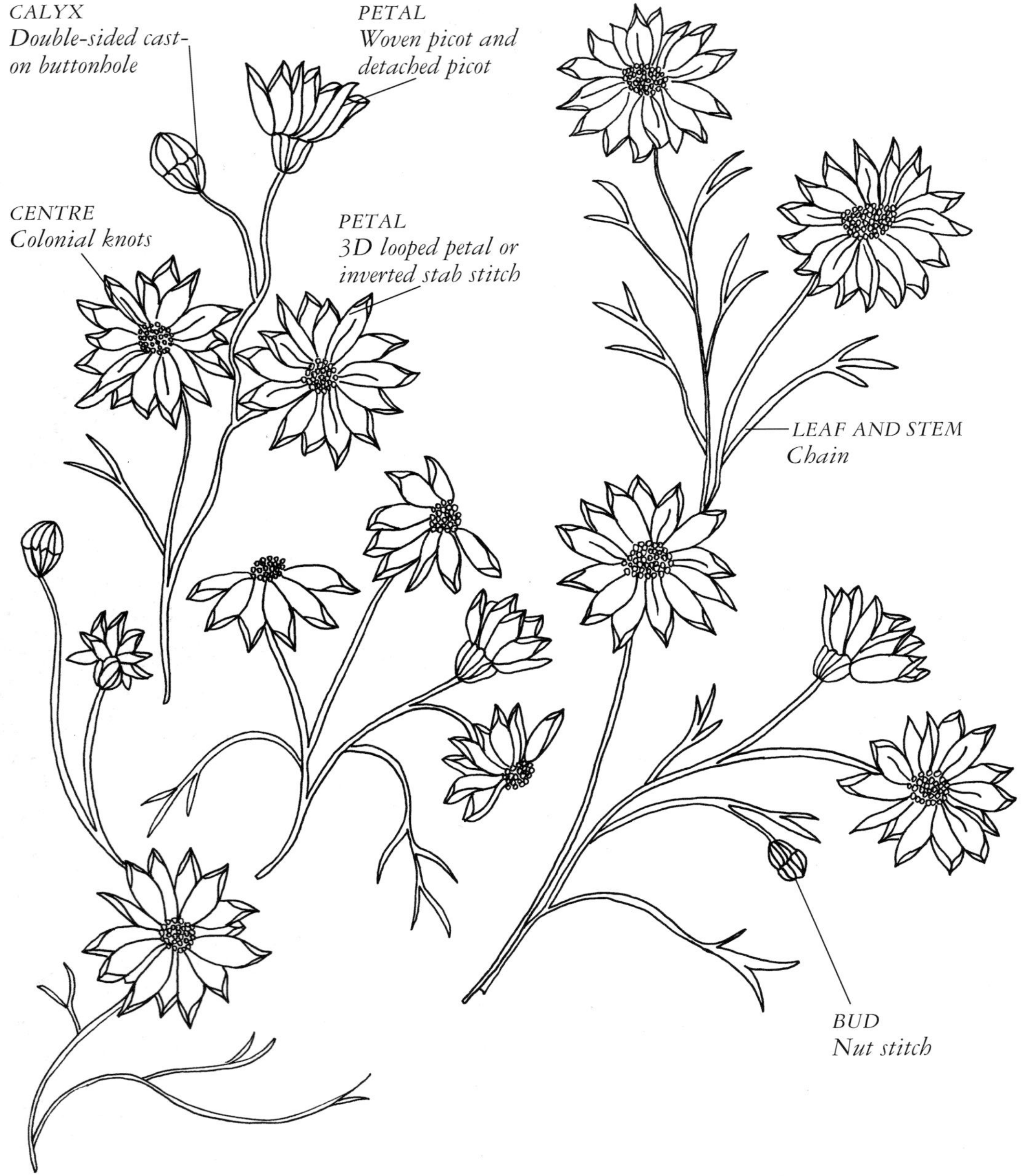

CALYX
Double-sided cast-on buttonhole

PETAL
Woven picot and detached picot

CENTRE
Colonial knots

PETAL
3D looped petal or inverted stab stitch

LEAF AND STEM
Chain

BUD
Nut stitch

Cream on Cream

Raw silk daisies on a moiré background. Manipulate the petals onto the fabric using the 3D looped petal method but only perforate the fabric to begin and end. *(see Portfolio of Stitches and Sketches)*

Hold each petal in place with a matching colonial knot and fill the centr with colonial knots in golden yellow floss (DMC 3046) in two strands. The fine petals are in chain stitch in ecru floss (DMC 739) in two strand

MOIRÉ *Raw silk daisies on moiré background fabric.* (Paulette Hodes)

smaller daisies are in woven picot and detached woven picot, while the ls are in nut stitch, all in ecru floss (DMC 739) in two strands. The stems leaves are in chain in green floss (DMC 3022, 642 and 3024) and the yxes are double sided cast-on buttonhole. *(See the crewel stitch glossary for all crewel stitches)*

silk daisies on jade are based on the same design as the cream, raw daisies.

SILK DAISIES ON JADE – *The petals are 7mm wide silk, the calyxes double-sided cast-on buttonhole and the stems are in chain.* (Madge Wulfsohn)

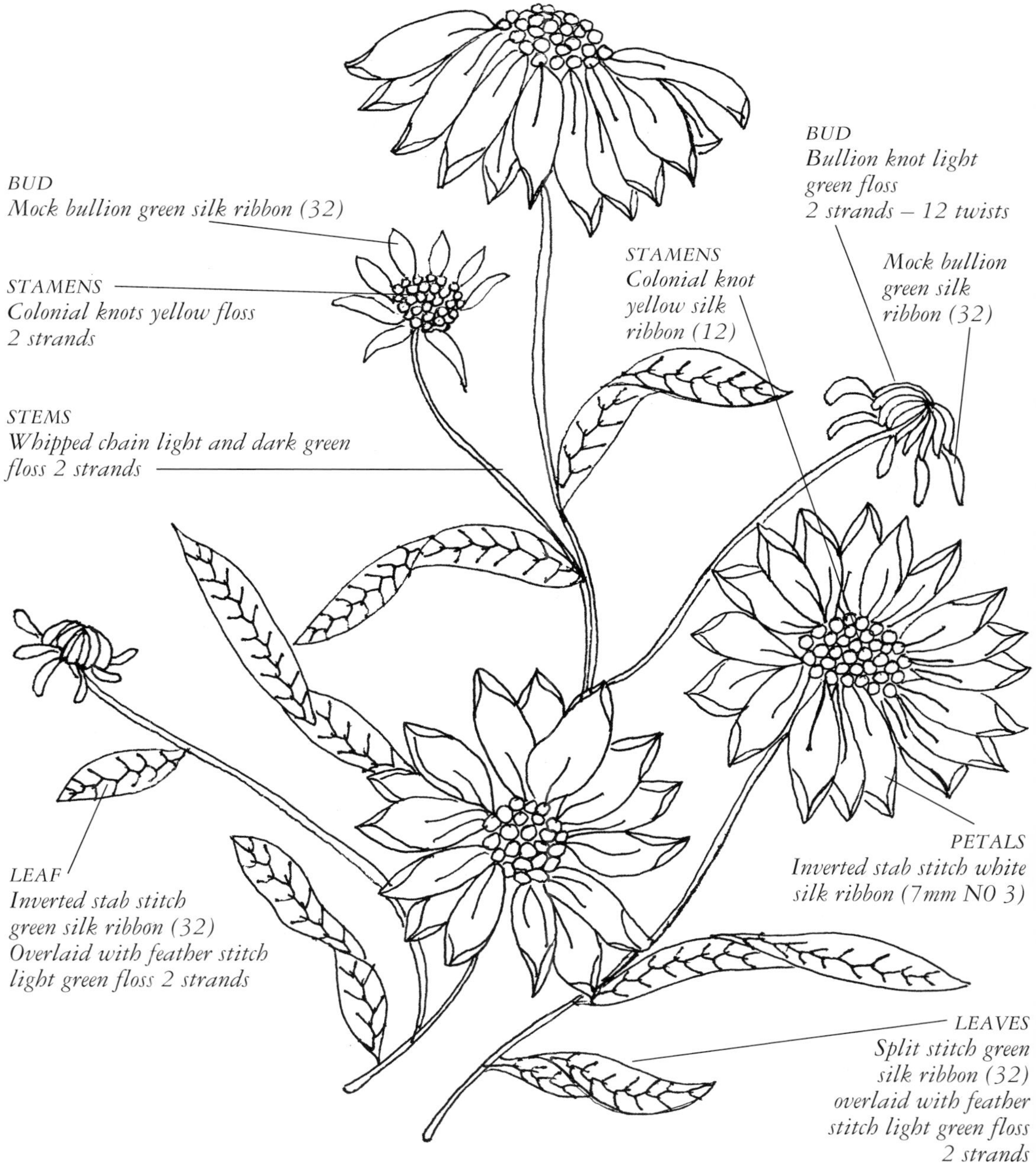

BUD
Mock bullion green silk ribbon (32)

STAMENS
Colonial knots yellow floss
2 strands

STEMS
Whipped chain light and dark green
floss 2 strands

LEAF
Inverted stab stitch
green silk ribbon (32)
Overlaid with feather stitch
light green floss 2 strands

STAMENS
Colonial knot
yellow silk
ribbon (12)

BUD
Bullion knot light
green floss
2 strands – 12 twists

Mock bullion
green silk
ribbon (32)

PETALS
Inverted stab stitch white
silk ribbon (7mm NO 3)

LEAVES
Split stitch green
silk ribbon (32)
overlaid with feather
stitch light green floss
2 strands

Silk Ribbon cosmos *(Rachelle Drijian)*

A field of white, rosy-pink and crimson cosmos, Northern Transvaal – inspiration for the creative sou

Victoriana and Precious Pieces in Fine Threads

A tissue box cover, lavender bag and tiny framed picture reflect the gentleness of a bye-gone era. Soft pastel silk ribbon flowers are worked into a Battenberg lace tissue box cover. The lavender bag is adorned with pale pink bullion roses. The miniature picture is a posy of bullion roses, lazy daisy and colonial knot forget-me-nots in one strand of embroidery floss.

Tissue box, lavender bag and miniature picture.
(Sharon Frittelli, Sandra Caister and Ann Foulner)

ANTIQUE HANDKERCHIEF CASE – courtesy of Margot Gawith.
Gold thread has been couched onto the satin background to create the word 'handkerchiefs' The silk ribbon roses are still intact almost ninety years later. The variegated silk was worked onto the background in folded triangles to create the burgundy rose.

Right: MANTEL CLOCK – *Silk ribbon wreath of flowers* (Carmen Isaacs)

WREATH OF FLOWERS
pink and jade variation.
(Leone Segal)

WREATH OF FLOWERS
Pink and jade – detail. This detail shows whipped spider's web roses and 3D looped petal daisies.

MANTEL CLOCK

Trace the design onto a rich moiré taffeta background. Begin by embroidering the twisted ribbon in raised stem in two strands of golden yellow floss. Interlace the ribbon with silk ribbon and crewel flower combinations – roses, lilac, lavender and daisies *(see Sweet Sixteen and a Floral ABC).* This clock face can be made up in different colour variations.

BLOSSOM BRANCH Flystitch and colonial knots

ROSES Woven spider's web

LILAC Bullions

LEAF Bullion

LAVENDAR Feather stitch foliage and bullion blooms

TWISTED RIBBON WREATH Raised stem

LEAF Lazy daisy

3D LOOPED DAISY

FLUTED/RUCHED PETALS

LEAF Inverted stab stitch

ROSEBUD BRANCH Stab stitch

STEM Backstitch

Antique Embroidered Pincushion or Lavender Bags

Materials

- Two 30 x 30cm seeded cotton (front and back of pincushion)
- One 30 x 30cm muslin
- No 8 crewel needle
- Embroidery floss
- Ecru ribbon
- Ecru lace
- Plastic hanger ring
- Inside pincushion

Instructions

A must for every creative needle crafter ; a delightful pincushion/lavender bag to play with the versatility of basic crewel stitches combined to form floral shapes.
Trace the design onto the seeded cotton by placing the fabric over the illustration provided. Mark the design directly onto the fabric with a soft pencil. A normal HB is fine but press fairly lightly.
Baste the muslin and top fabric together. (The muslin gives body and a foundation for beginning and ending neatly.)
Insert the fabric into an embroidery ring.
Most of the embroidery should be done in one strand of embroidery thread.
Work the larger flowers first, and then fill in the spaces with smaller flowers.
Use the sketch as your guide and create a pot pourri of your favourite combinations.
The butterfly outline is in colonial knots in candlewicking thread No. 8.

How to Make Up a Pincushion *(See Portfolio of Stitches and Sketches)*

Once all the embroidery is complete, cut out the circle on the solid line. Join the length of lace, run a gathering thread along the inner edge and pull up to fit the circle. Stitch the lace to the fabric. Cut out the 2 half backs using the pattern provided. Make a hem on the straight side of each half circle.
Cover the plastic hanger ring with buttonhole using ecru thread. Thread the ribbon through the ring and back into place behind the lace.
Assemble the pincushion with the right sides together, lace and ribbon facing inwards. Machine stitch around the circle. Trim and turn through to the right side.

To Make an Inner Cushion

Cut two pieces of calico the size of the sketch provided.
Stitch them together leaving a small opening for stuffing. Trim and turn through. Stuff with soft wadding and slip hem the opening.
Pop the inner cushion into the pincushion.
For a bit of fun you could put a small sachet of pot pourri into the cushion.

LAVENDER BAG *Circle of Flowers* (Bridget Price)

A Pot Pourri of Lavender Bags and Pincushions

These designs are in single strand crewel flowers using bullions, buttonholes and french knots.

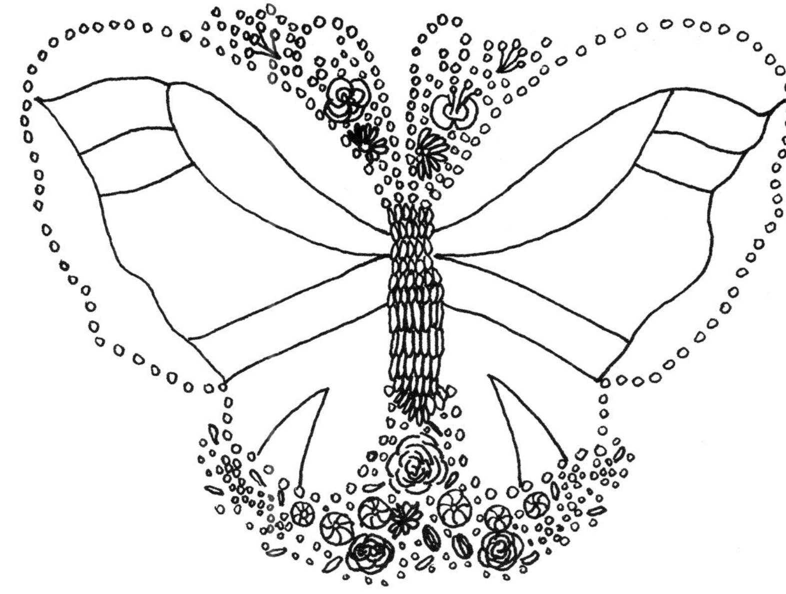

Left: LAVENDER BAG
Tiny posy
(Bridget Price)

Right: LAVENDER BAG
Butterfly
(Bridget Price)

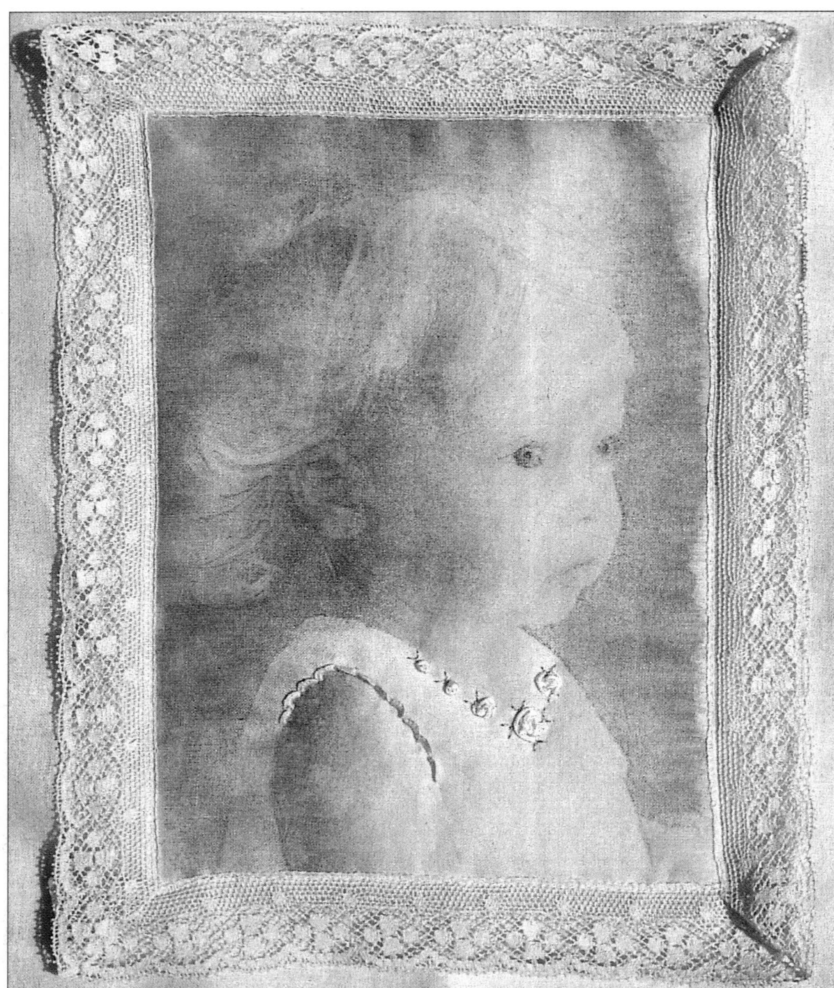

Baby Portrait on Antique Handkerchief
A charming way of enjoying Grandmother's handkerchief collection. Transfer the baby portrait from a photocopy onto the handkerchief. Place the photocopy, face down onto the handkerchief and rub the back gently with cotton wool soaked with thinners. This will transfer the image onto the fabric. Edge the portrait with antique lace and add a few embroidered details to the child's garments. *(Lesley Turpin-Delport)*

A Signature Pillow
All the embroidery is in one or two strands. Colonial knots and extended french knots form the large roses. The rosebuds and leaves are in romanian and extended french knots. The four-petal pink daisies are in buttonhole and extended french knots in one strand. The gyp-sophila and forget-me-nots are in colonial knots in one strand. The lattice work is in blue s thread, in raised stem, with golden-yellow, silk thread bars of double-sided cast-on buttonho Finish off your pillow with a raised stem signature of pink silk in one strand. *(Ethel Walt)*

An Introduction to Ribbon Embroidery

The exciting part of ribbon embroidery is the speed of the technique. Enjoy the free style element of ribbon embroidery and create your own magic.

I love combining different media and feel you should experiment with the techniques using a wide range of ribbons such as satin, silk, rayon, velvet or taffeta.

Satin ribbon can be softened with touches of crewel embroidery and silk ribbon foliage. Fine satin ribbon does pull through open weave fabrics such as even weave or coarse linen and wool. See the step-by-step instructions of how to make cabbage roses and large, flamboyant satin ribbon roses. *(See page 70–73 in Portfolio of Sketches and Stitches)*

Basket of Roses

Satin ribbon roses snuggle into 3D silk ribbon daisies and colonial knot branches of heather. The basket weave is created in cast-on buttonhole in two strands of ginger floss. *(Denise Crain)* Below is the detail showing the cabbage rose (tab method) in satin ribbon 10mm wide.

Right: **The Great Gatsby**

Flamboyant satin ribbon roses are seen in all their glory adorning exciting head gear. *Laverne Hardwick, Elaine Walker and Evonne Ghemo-Tudorich, Irene McCarthy.*

ANTIQUE EMBELLISHMENT

A wreath of satin ribbon roses, silk ribbon daisies, colonial knot gypsophila and french knot heather is worked in striking colours onto an antique handkerchief. *(Susan Sittig)*

Garland of Fuchsias

A Few Fuchsias

The gentle Oriental charm of fuchsias is re-created by manipulating silk ribbon to form a garland of flowers, ideal for a tea cosy, cushion, clock face or framed picture.

FUCHSIA GARLAND OR CASCADING SPRAY
Fine fuchsias in silk ribbon embroidery.
(*Cushion* – Di Thompson,
Cosy – Anne Neill
Picture – Eleanor Jubiler)

A Fuchsia Garland or Cascading Spray

Materials

- Background fabric, bottle green or white (40 x 40cm)
- Muslin (40 x 40cm)
- Silk ribbon
- A selection of embroidery floss
- Crewel needle
- Chenille needle

Instructions

Position the cotton fabric over the design and lightly sketch the design onto the background. If you choose bottle green fabric, use dressmaker's carbon to transfer the design onto your fabric.

Basic Fuchsia Sketch

Study the labelled sketch and the photographs and begin with the embroidered stems in whipped backstitch, using two strands of green floss for the backstitch and then whip in one strand of rose pink floss. The fine stems are in one strand of rose pink floss in backstitch. The pedicel is in two strands of green floss in bullions (6/8 twists); two bullions for buds and small blooms ; three bullions for large blooms.
Now study the silk ribbon basics, *(see in The Portfolio of Sketches and Stitches)* labelled sketch and stitch glossary and create the fuchsia blooms and buds.
The leaves are inverted stab stitch in green silk, secured with a rose pink stab stitch. Complete the flowers with stamens and pistil, in extended french knots in ecru, rose pink and pale apricot floss, in one or two strands.
The small fuchsia designs *(Garland, Spray and sampler)* are in 3.5 mm wide silk ribbon, while the large fuchsias are in 7mm wide silk ribbon *(White marshmallow fuchsias – see pictures on page 38)*.

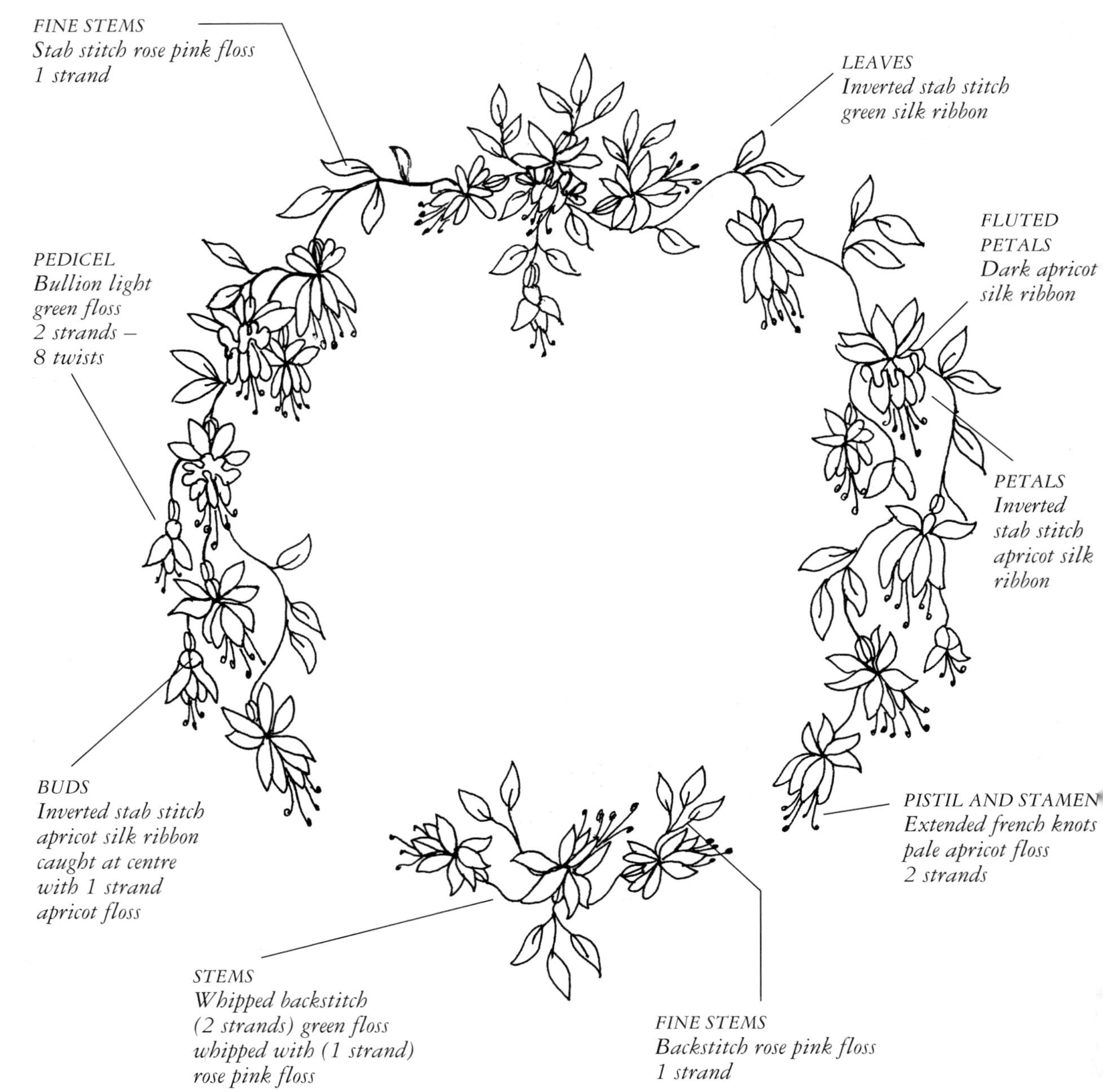

FUCHSIA SAMPLER
Select your favourite fuchsia shapes and colours and create your own sampler of cascading flowers and buds on a pure silk background fabric. (Di Thompson)

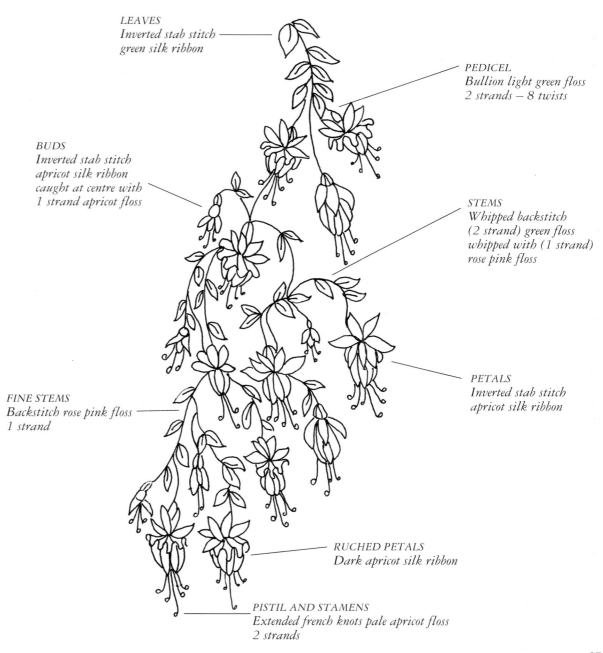

LEAVES
Inverted stab stitch green silk ribbon

PEDICEL
Bullion light green floss 2 strands – 8 twists

BUDS
Inverted stab stitch apricot silk ribbon caught at centre with 1 strand apricot floss

STEMS
Whipped backstitch (2 strand) green floss whipped with (1 strand) rose pink floss

PETALS
Inverted stab stitch apricot silk ribbon

FINE STEMS
Backstitch rose pink floss 1 strand

RUCHED PETALS
Dark apricot silk ribbon

PISTIL AND STAMENS
Extended french knots pale apricot floss 2 strands

Inspiration for White Marshmallow Fuchsias
These extravagant fuchsias were blooming in all their splendour in the Northern Transvaal, South Africa.

Right: **White Marshmallow Pink and White Fuchsias**
Notice the fluted/ruched petals on this design in 7mm wide, pale pink silk ribbon (No. 157). *(Di Thompson)*

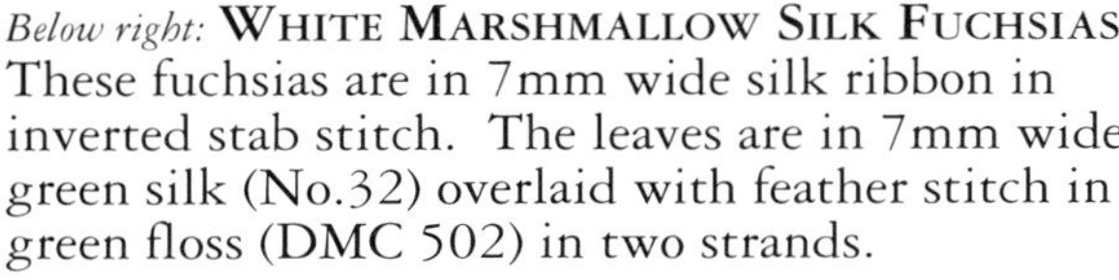

Below right: **White Marshmallow Silk Fuchsias**
These fuchsias are in 7mm wide silk ribbon in inverted stab stitch. The leaves are in 7mm wide green silk (No.32) overlaid with feather stitch in green floss (DMC 502) in two strands.

WHITE MARSHMALLOW FUCHSIA

WHITE MARSHMALLOW PINK AND WHITE FUCHSIA

Creepers and Crawlies

Creepers with their showy blooms immediately suggest interpretation in silk ribbon, paint and crewel embroidery. Without the butterflies, bees and tiny creatures we would not have these splendid blooms. So last but not least, these important creatures are given a show.

BUTTERFLIES IN FULL FLIGHT (Paulette Hodes)

Wisteria Sinensis "Alba"

The wisteria has been lightly painted in white and shades of green on a pale green linen background. Create the buds in 3.5mm silk, playing with a variety of stitches – stab stitch, lazy daisy, bullion-lazy daisy combinations and mock bullions. The calyxes are lazy daisy in green silk ribbon (Nos. 32 and 33). The blooms are in two shades of white silk ribbon (Nos. 1 and 3) ; with the upper petals in inverted stab stitch (7mm) and the lower petals in stab stitch or lazy daisy (3.5mm). Manipulate and form the upper petals into a "bonnet like" shape and secure them with bullions in one strand of pale pink and two strands of golden yellow floss. (DMC 224 and 3046). The stems are long bullions, created on a straw needle, in green floss (DMC 502 and 501) in two strands. The leaves are in inverted stab stitch in green silk (Nos. 32 and 33) overlaid with feather stitch in two strands of green floss (DMC 503).

WISTERIA SINENSIS 'ALBA' (Lesley Turpin-Delport)

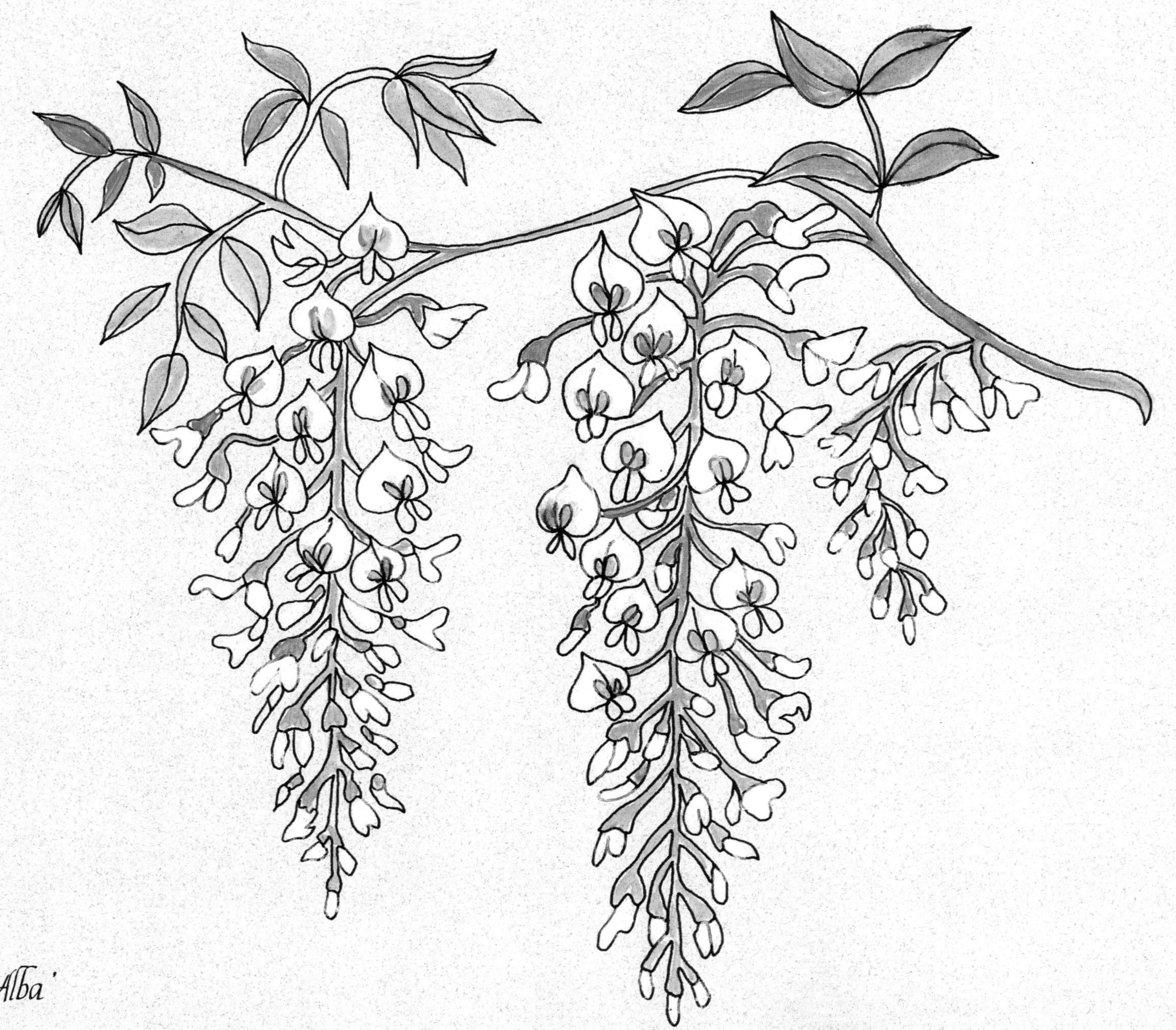

Wisteria Sinensis 'Alba'

Honeysuckle with a Floral Braided Border

Gingham Cross-stitch with Silk Ribbon

Create your cross-stitches on alternate white squares of the gingham (see example in photograph).
The crosses are made in three strands of rose pink embroidery floss (DMC 223).
Make all the cross-stitches using the corner grid as your guide.

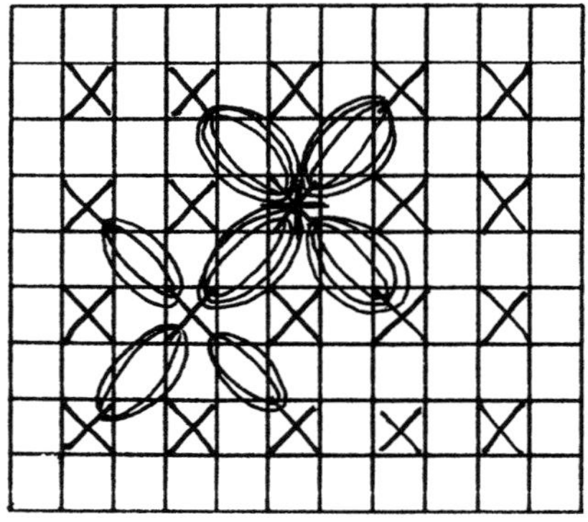

(Count your checks carefully to see that you create perfect flowers and leaves at the corners).
Now begin your silk ribbon flowers using yellow silk ribbon (No. 14) following the diagrams for petal direction.
For a bulky flower, work each petal twice.

The centres are a single cross-stitch in bright pink silk ribbon (No. 128). The leaves are worked in the same way as the flowers in green silk ribbon (No. 32)

Enjoy the potential of gingham cross-stitch and create many different designs by linking the crosses in different directions.

HONEYSUCKLE ON GINGHAM WITH A FLORAL BRAIDED BORDER
Create your honeysuckle branch using the photographs and painting as your guide and follow th gingham cross-stitch with silk ribbon instructions for the floral braided border.
(Nicola Delport and Julie Lazarus)

ONEYSUCKLE FLOWER DETAILS
he bloom is a mixture of split stitch, bullion-lazy daisy mbination and stab stitch. The calyx is mock bullion in een silk ribon and the stamens and pistil are whipped ckstitch and bullion in two strands of pink and green oss. (Nanda Dos Santos)

Honeysuckle at Orchards Road

Above inset: **Spring Jasmine Cushion**
(Anne Neill)

Right inset: **Detail of Jasmine Cushion**
(Anne Neill)

The Pergola Silk ribbon roses tumble over an old fashioned pergola, surrounded by summer flowers in silk and crewel embroidery. *(Lynn Road)*

low: Erica and Bumble Bees nestling in evening primrose
rmanent marker, soft paint and a dash of silk ribbon on white linen is sure be a success. *(Lesley Turpin-Delport)*

p right: Daisies and Forget-me-nots intertwined
ny bullion bees swirl within the floral garland. *(Linda de Luca)*

ttom right: Gingham and Gold
umble bees on a quilted background are complimented by a bold gingham ll and golden rayon ribbon bows. The bees are in silk ribbon in colonial ots and turkey work (tufting) in floss. *(Renske Biddulph)*

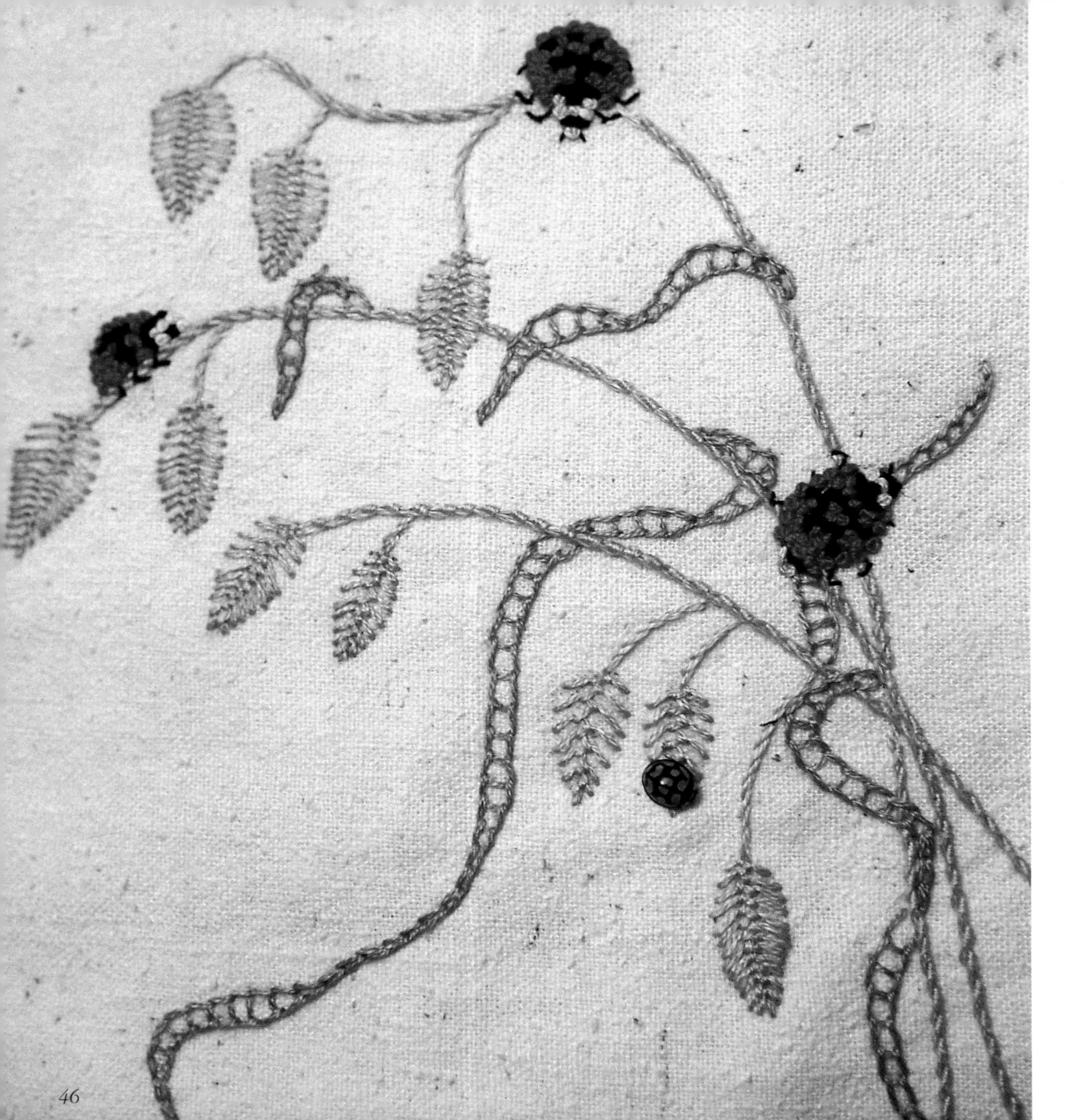

A Small Miracle

Tiny creatures of the animal kingdom always hold a fascination for me.

A design of waving grasses had to be embroidered with a couple of ladybirds for that extra dimension and dash of colour. The raw silk background fabric and wheat coloured grasses just needed the bright red and black knots of the little beetle.

While photographing this design for the book, a tiny flying creature descended onto the leaf. I could not believe what I saw. Small is beautiful and I quickly focussed the camera. A ladybird, in all its glory had joined the shoot. It lingered just a moment and then flew off into the garden beyond, perhaps remembering the nursery rhyme: 'Ladybird, ladybird, fly away home .....'

I had captured a small miracle on camera.

Ladybirds in the grass – a small miracle
The grasses are cretan stitch and open chain while the ladybirds are french knots and stab stitch.
(Renske Biddulph)

Fynbos (Heliophilia elongata) at Sedgefield · Cape · December 1993 ·

Fragile Fynbos

Fynbos (Fine bush) is the natural vegetation of the southern and south western Cape Province, South Africa.
These indigenous plants have a delicate beauty which lends itself to interpretation in silk ribbon and fine threads.
Around the area of Sedgefield on the Garden Route, I have watched the fine grasses and shrubs bloom throughout the different seasons. Each time one imagines you have seen them all, there is a new discovery.
A delicate balance is evident between the plants and animals that co-exist in harmony in this floral kingdom. The tortoise, is peculiar to this area. I just had to include this precious creature in our embroidery story.

HELIOPHILIA (ELONGATA)
Inspiration – Sedgefield, Cape, December 1993.

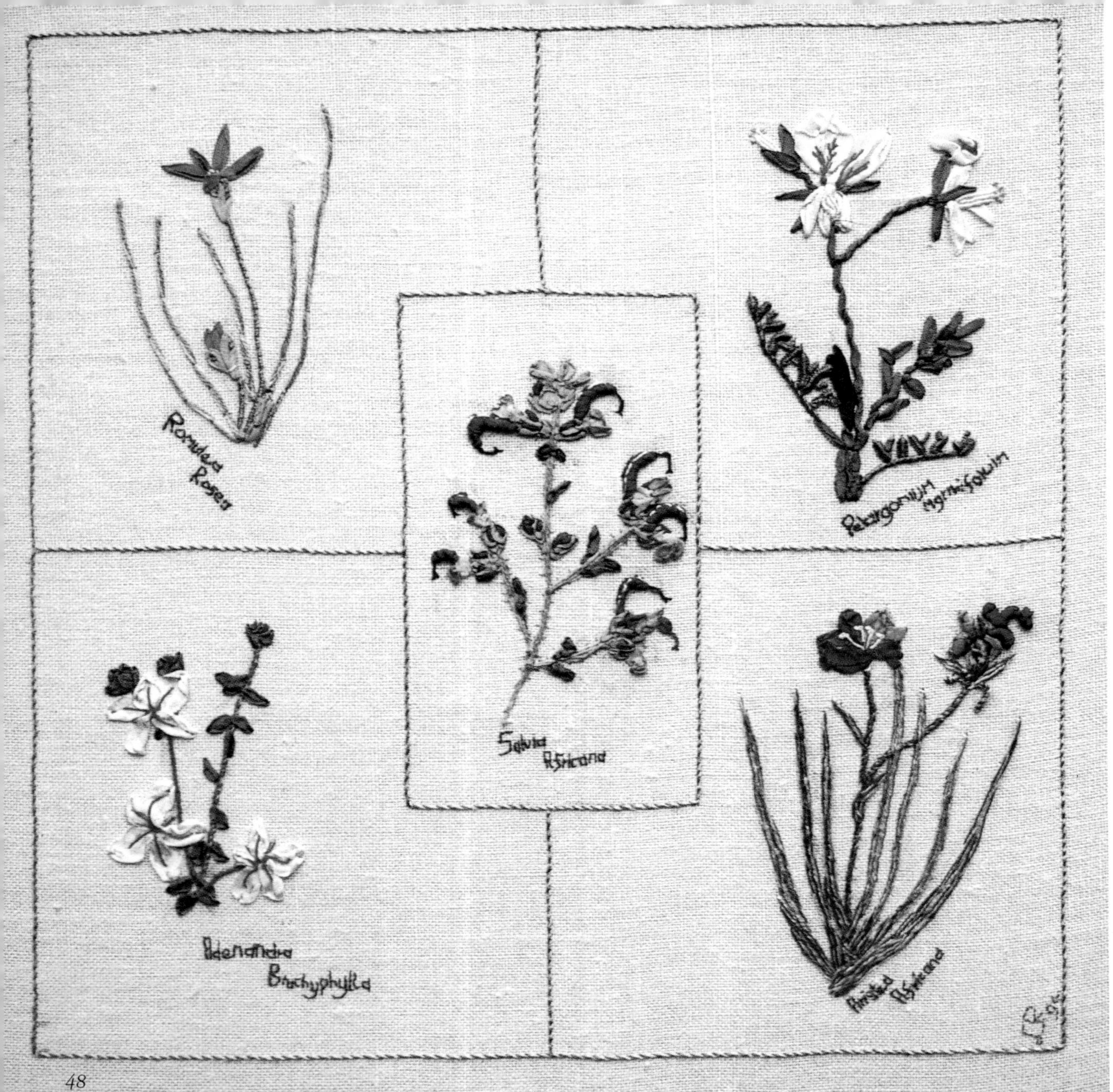

FYNBOS QUINTET
Salvia africana, Romulea rosea, Pelargonium myrrhifoliu Adenandra brachyphylla and Aristea africana – silk rib and crewel embroidery in perfect harmony. (Lynn Read)

SALVIA ELONGATA LUTEA
(Detail of Fynbos inspiration) Sedgefield, Cape, December 1993 – wild Sage.

CREWEL DAISIES ON PLAID (Renske Biddulph)

BARELY THE SIZE OF A DAISY – *young tortoise*

FYNBOS DAISIES IN SILK RIBBON (Madge Wulfsohn)

EMBROIDERED TORTOISE
Work in progress. The fabric applique is embroidered in place with metallic thread, silk ribbon and stranded cott The different fibres give an exciting texture to the design. (Madge Wulfsohn)

STAPELIA GRANDIFLORA – *Succulent.* (Di Thompsor

RSA
Gestandaardiseerde pos
Standardised mail
Stapelia grandiflora
Hein Botha
1992

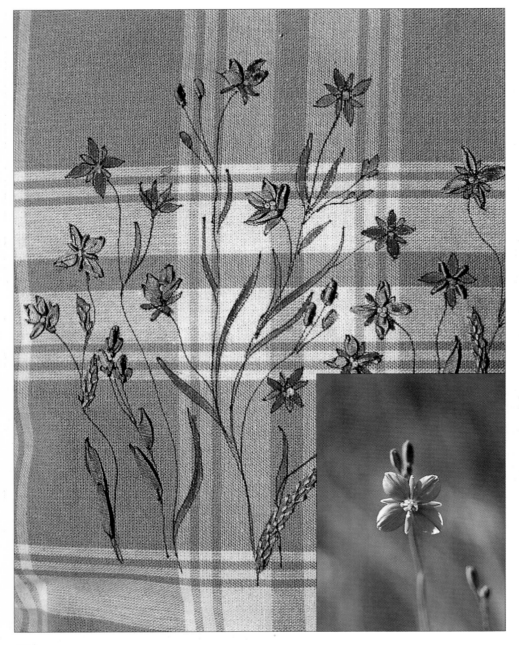

Pelargonium Inquinans

This plant, which grows wild along the east coast of southern Africa is one of the parents of the vivid scarlet garden hybrids grown around the world; often mistakenly called geraniums – it was taken from South Africa to England and cultivated there as early as 1714. African tribal people use parts of the plant as a headache and cold remedy. In the picture below, the scarlet petals are in 7mm rayon ribbon, balanced by hand appliquéd leaves.*(Di Thompson)*

Left: BLUE SILK BLOOMS ON PLAID – DETAIL (Lesley Turpin-Delport)
Inspired by the beautiful Heliophilia elongata flowering in Sedgefield in December, blue silk ribbon and paint on plaid was an exciting interpretation for this delicate fynbos plant.

Left inset: HELIOPHILIA *(Elongata) Bloom*
The single flower with its four petals and green calyx is striking in its sheer simplicity.

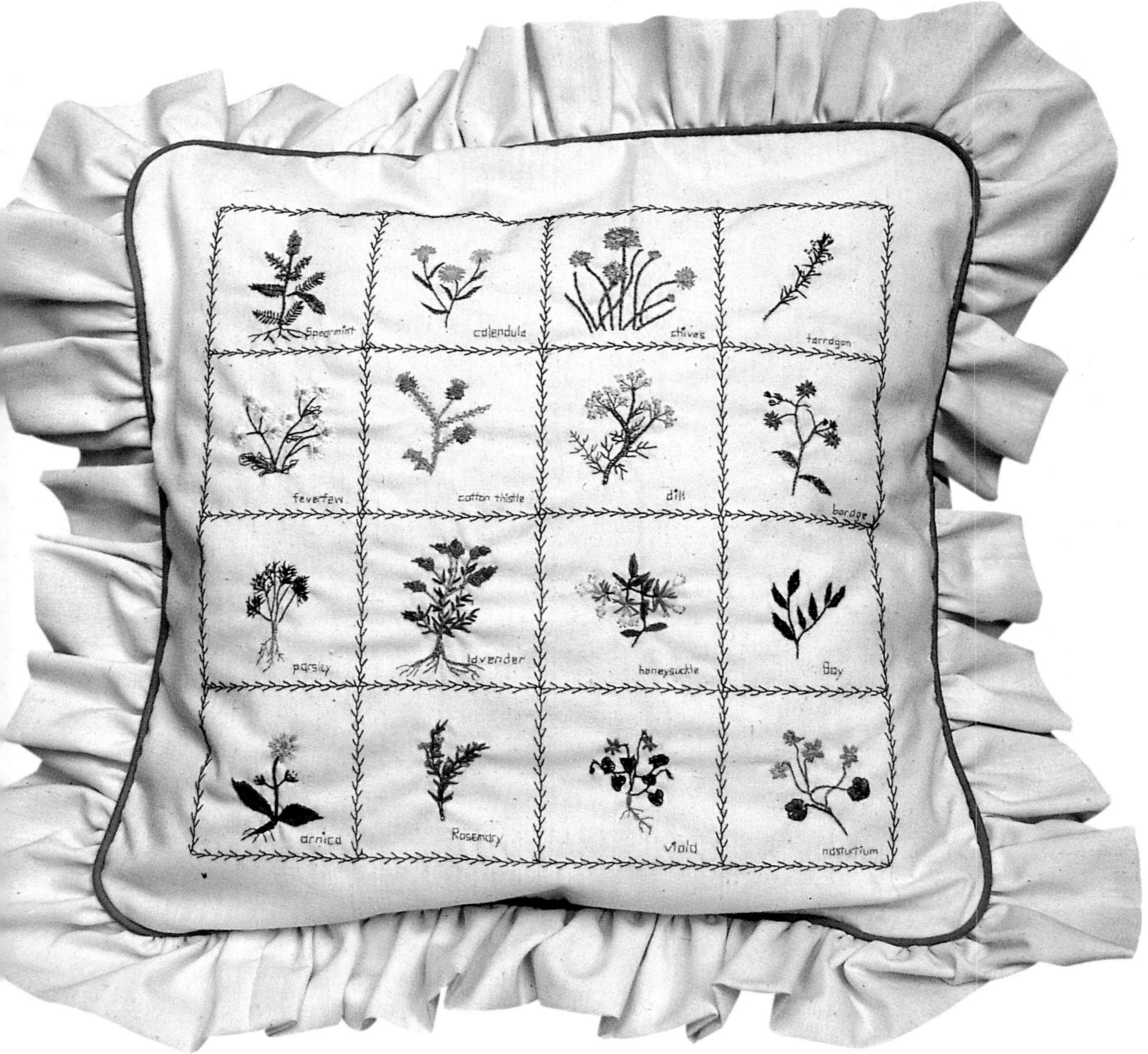

The Herb Garden

What wonderful delicate flowers can be found amongst the foliage of garden herbs. Here are sixteen tiny herbs in crewel stitches, in one and two strands of floss, for the needlecrafter to add to the floral vocabulary. With a knowledge of sixteen basic herbs at your fingertips, you can create your own miniature herb gardens in pots and window boxes.

MINIATURE HERB SAMPLER CUSHION (Sandra Caister)
This is a mix and match design with 'Sweet Sixteen' spring and summer flowers.

THISTLE IN MAGOEBOESKLOOF
Northern Transvaal, South Africa
The inspiration for the cotton thistle in the herb sampler.

A Miniature Herb Garden

The herbs that appear in the miniature herb garden are: marigolds, rosemary, nasturtiums, indian pinks, bergamot, borage, dill, lavender, mint, basil, chives, parsley, sage and sprouts.
Herb gardens are fun to create and make delightful samplers, cushions etc.
The design below was adapted from a delightful sketch of a herb garden in "A Modern Herbal" (Edited by Violet Stevenson – Treasure Press).

Pot and Urn Detail
These charming pots are given added dimensions with trapunto quilting, by pushing small quantities of wadding into the cavity in between the muslin foundation and the top fabric. The foliage depicted in the picture above, is in woven picot (front plant) and wheatear stitch (back plant).*(Anne Neill)*

Bergamot – Detail from a Miniature Herb Garden
The blooms of the Bergamot are cast-on buttonhole and split stitch in 2 strands of deep red floss. (DMC 347). The stamens are yellow extended French knots in 1 strand. The leaves are Romanian in 2 strands of green floss with a central vein in plum overcast stem (DMC 315) *(Anne Neill)*

VARIATION ON A THEME

A miniature herb garden. The same layout with different colours and stitches – creates a unique herb garden. *(Sheila Hill)*

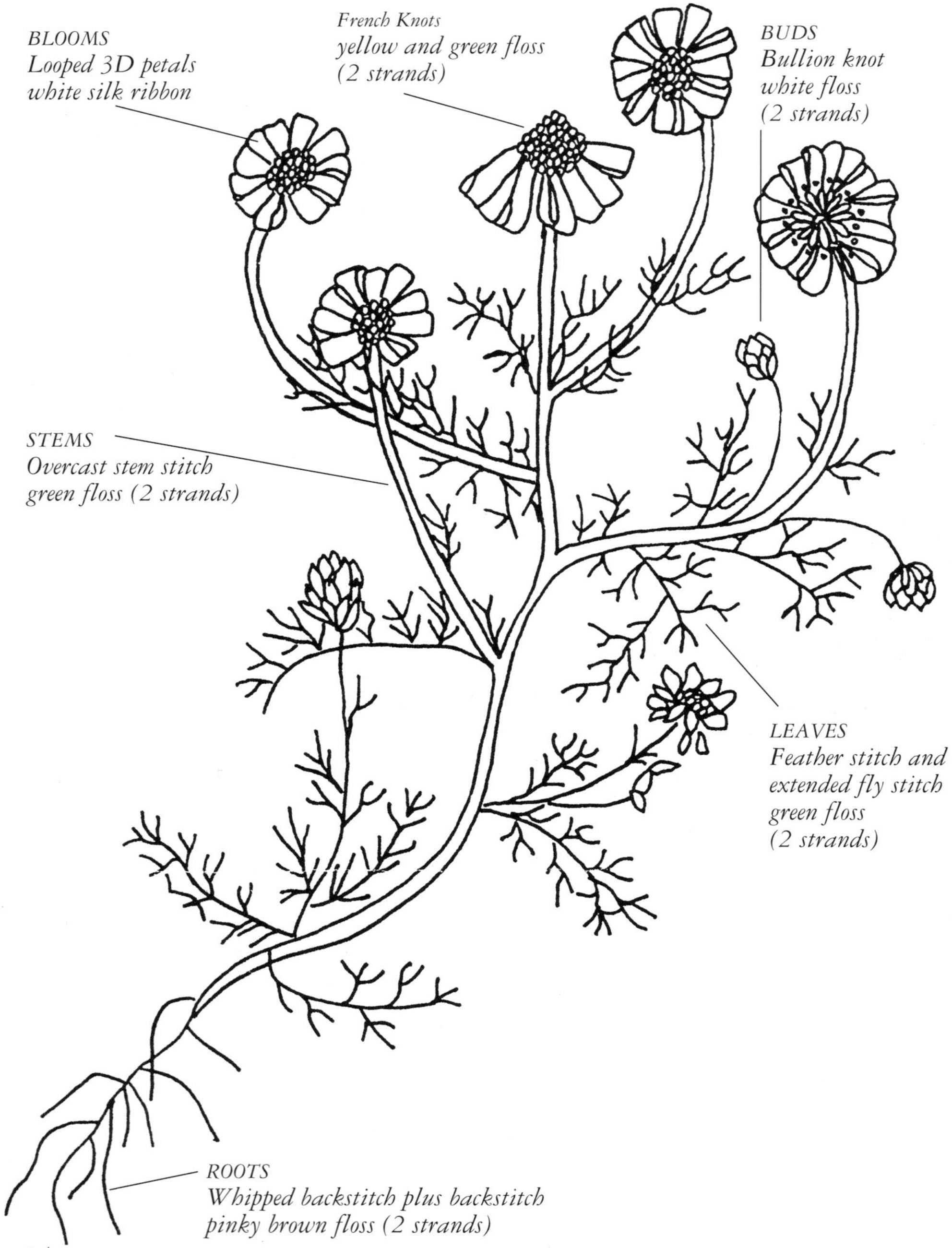

CAMOMILE CUSHION

3D silk ribbon petals and fine floss embroidery foliage are glamourised on eau-de-nil moiré taffeta (Sandra Caister)

The Enchanted Gardens

The final chapter is a culmination of all the ideas and techniques which have appeared in the previous chapters. Go out and re-discover a quiet corner, a formal rose garden, a shady glen.
Joy in the quiet reverie and create your own enchanted garden.

"I know a bank where the wild thyme blows,
Where oxslips and the nodding violet grows
Quite over-canopied with luscious woodbine,
With sweet musk-roses, and with eglantine"

William Shakespeare from
"A Midsummer Nights Dream"

Terracotta Terrace · Colenso Road · Cape

Hand Painted Homestead *(Felicity Goldstein)*
Topiary trees, arums, daffodils, fuchsias, shasta daisies, lavender, alyssum, acanthus and flowering shrubs are worked in floss, silk, perle and silk ribbon.

An Enchanted Garden *(Lesley Turpin-Delport)*
Mixed media of paint, silk and crewel work combine to create an enchanted garden of lattice, pergolas, terracotta pots and tubs spilling with free-style embroidered flowers.

Opposite page: **Twin Tubs in a Lighter Shade of Pale**

Ink in the fine lines of the garden with a permanent marker and paint the terracotta pots and flowers with fabric paint. Add the finishing touches in mixed threads and silk ribbon for an English country garden of hydrangeas, arums, snowdrops, roses, agapanthus, alysum, white wisteria, morning glory and flowering lemon trees. The lattice has been quilted using a single strand of green floss in chain stitch. *(See Textile Sandwich in Sweet Sixteen page 18)*
(Eleanor Jubiler)

Left: **Down the Path**

After a journey through the pages of "Just Flowers", learning about the different techniques and methods of creating flowers, meander down your garden path and discover a corner of your own garden and re-create it in mixed media.
(Avril Walsh)

Below is the original inspiration for "Down the garden path" at Orchards Road.

Twin tubs in a Lighter Shade of Pale. *(Eleanor Jubiler)*

A TOPIARY TREE *(Ann Foulner)*

Create a topiary tree on an antique pink, moiré taffeta background. The embroidery is essentially in silk ribbon techniques with the tendrils, stem and a few leaves in crewel stitches. Study the labelled sketch and enjoy the quick and tactile effect of silk ribbon embroidery.

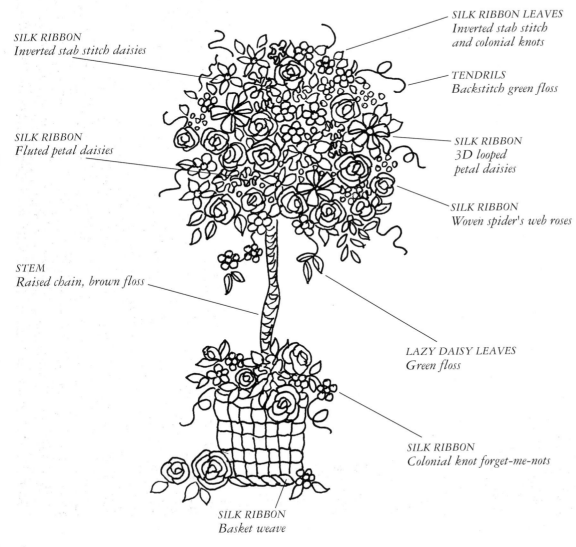

SILK RIBBON
Inverted stab stitch daisies

SILK RIBBON
Fluted petal daisies

STEM
Raised chain, brown floss

SILK RIBBON LEAVES
Inverted stab stitch and colonial knots

TENDRILS
Backstitch green floss

SILK RIBBON
3D looped petal daisies

SILK RIBBON
Woven spider's web roses

LAZY DAISY LEAVES
Green floss

SILK RIBBON
Colonial knot forget-me-nots

SILK RIBBON
Basket weave

A TOPIARY TREE (Ann Foulner)

A TOPIARY CUSHION. (Sandra Caister) *Try a canary yellow background fabric with a topiary tree in blue, bottle green, plum and white silk ribbon.*

THE GARDEN BENCH
Mixed media – paint, silk and floss *(Sharon Frittelli)*

Top left: **ANOTHER INTERPRETATION OF THE GARDEN BENCH**
This version of the garden bench is in one and two strand crewel embroidery only. *(Gillian Smith)*

Lower left: **THE GARDEN POND**
A tiny snail observes the foliage of tufting, picot, wheatear and feather stitch. The minute stab stitch of the lawn unifies the design. *(Gillian Smith)*

Below: **A DELIGHTFUL TEDDY BEAR.**
Roses and daisies in silk ribbon and crewel turn a simple teddy bear into something very quaint. *(Val Lane)*

A Formal Garden

A formal garden presents a real challenge to the creative embroiderer. Imagine that you have seen an aerial view of the garden and interpret the design in geometric patterns by making a clever choice of stitches. An antique handkerchief has been used as a background with pale pink and eau-de-nil fabric underneath the handkerchief. Di has created a formal garden of creepers on a pergola, a maze, lily pond and beds of shrubs. All the stitches are in one or two strands of embroidery floss. *(Di Thompson)*

Below: **Garden Shrubs Seen from the Top**
Detail from a formal garden showing detached picot, tufting, bullion, cast-on buttonhole and a myriad of wonderful embroidery stitches in fine threads.

Portfolio
of
Sketches and Stitches

Working with Silk Ribbon

Embroidery with silk ribbon is fun and quick to do. The stitches used are the same as those used in traditional embroidery floss, but the silk ribbon gives the stitches exciting dimensions.
Keep the ribbon flat as it is threaded in and out of the fabric and control the tension on the ribbon and you will be thrilled with the result.

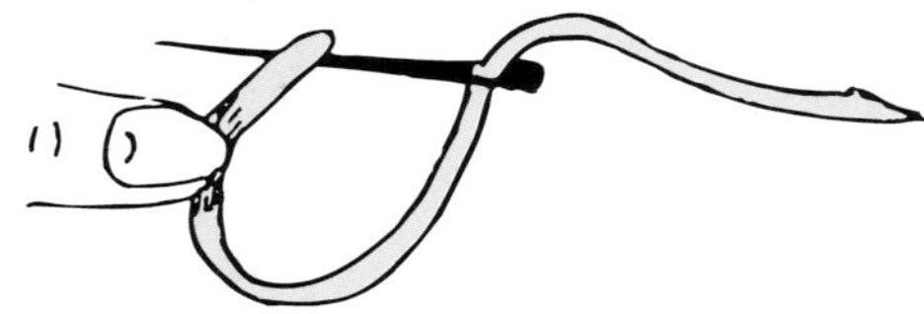

Length of Ribbon

Cut the ribbon at an angle of approx 30cm (12") in length. Too long a ribbon will fray and twist, which will not enhance your embroidery.

To thread the needle

Thread the ribbon through the eye of the needle, pull the ribbon through approx 2" (5cm) and pierce the ribbon approx 1cm ($^1/_2$") from the end. Pull the long end of the ribbon downwards until the ribbon locks into the eye of the needle. This prevents the needle from unthreading while you work.

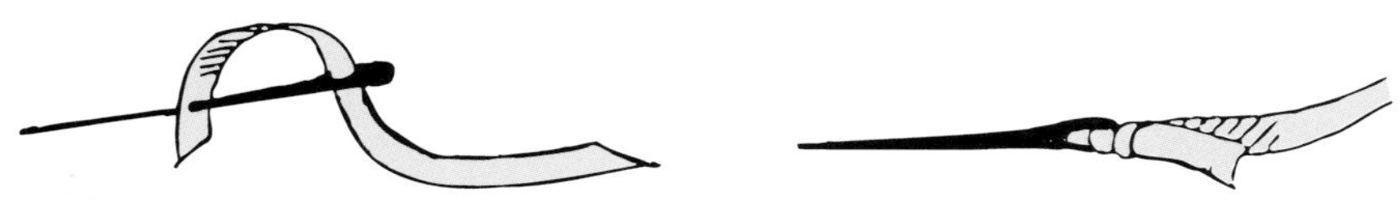

How to begin

I like to work with a muslin foundation behind the background fabric. This is not always necessary but usually gives the work more body and also allows for a neat ending. Begin by leaving a small tail hanging at the back of your work. As you make your first stitch, pierce the tail with the needle to secure the ribbon.

Some needlewomen find the tail securing difficult while doing tricky combinations. If this is the case make a small backstitch in the muslin foundation. Do not jump from one part of the design to another, as the colour might show through the background fabric, and you might cause a pucker. To prevent puckering, you should work with a small 3"(8cm) embroidery ring.

To finish off your stitch

Take the ribbon through to the back and work a small backstitch into the muslin foundation and through the ribbon. Be careful not to snag the embroidered ribbon in that area OR leave a tail which can be caught in, when the next thread is started.

Popular Stitches in Silk Ribbon

Stab stitch

These are single spaced stitches worked either in a regular or irregular manner. Sometimes the stitches are of varying size. The stitches should be neither too long nor too loose.

Inverted Stab stitch

Bring the needle through the background fabric and at the tip of the ribbon, pierce the ribbon and the fabric in the same movement. Pull the ribbon gently through forming a 'nipped' tip.

PLIT STITCH

Iake a single straight stitch. Now ring the needle up through the fabric, iercing through the centre of the titch from below, dividing the ribbon xactly in the middle. Repeat, forming neat line of stitches.

LY STITCH

Iake a satin stitch but come up in the entre of the stitch at a diagonal. Pull hrough and anchor the stitch with a mall tying stitch.

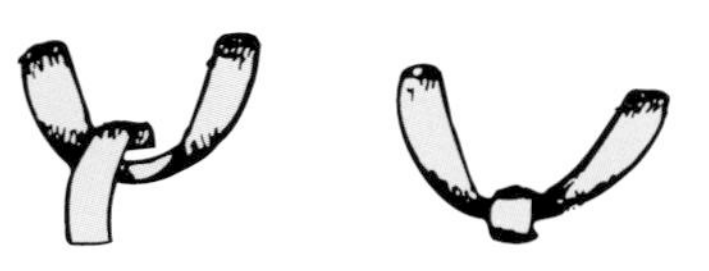

OLONIAL KNOT

ull the ribbon through the fabric. lace the needle under the ribbon, iding the needle from left to right. (1)

Vrap the ribbon over the top of the eedle from right to left creating a gure eight. (2)

nsert the needle into the fabric close where it emerged; pull the working bbon taut with your left hand so that firm tight knot is formed. (3)

ull the needle to the wrong side of the bric forming a colonial knot. ome up at the next dot. (4)

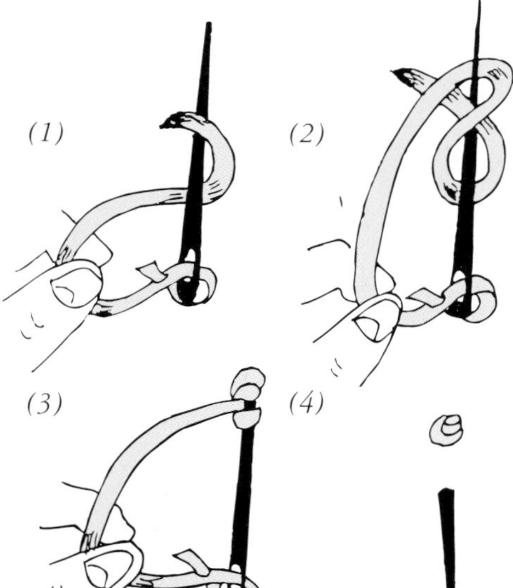

IRIS STITCH

Make a single chain stitch and anchor it with a small straight stitch. Bring the ribbon through the fabric on the lower right of the chain. Using the back of the needle, slip the ribbon under the base of the chain loop. Anchor the ribbon on the lower left of the chain stitch, re-entering the background at this point.
Make a yellow colonial knot or bullion in the centre of the chain stitch in two strands of floss.

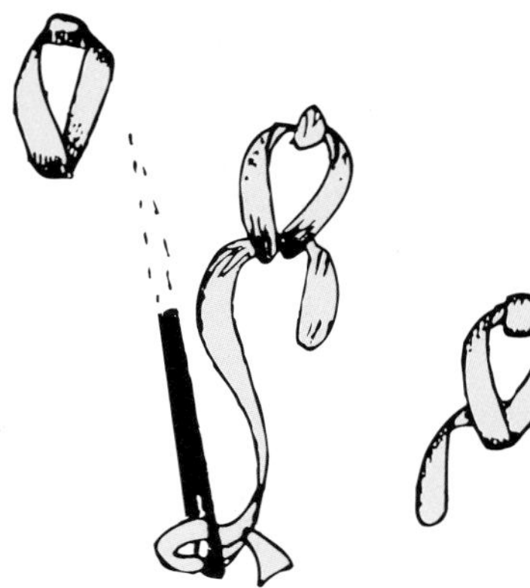

MOCK BULLION

Make a stab stitch as your foundation. Use the back of the needle and wrap the ribbon around the stab stitch, three or four times, moving along the stitch. Turn around the top of the stitch and wrap the stab stitch three or four times again, moving down the stitch length.

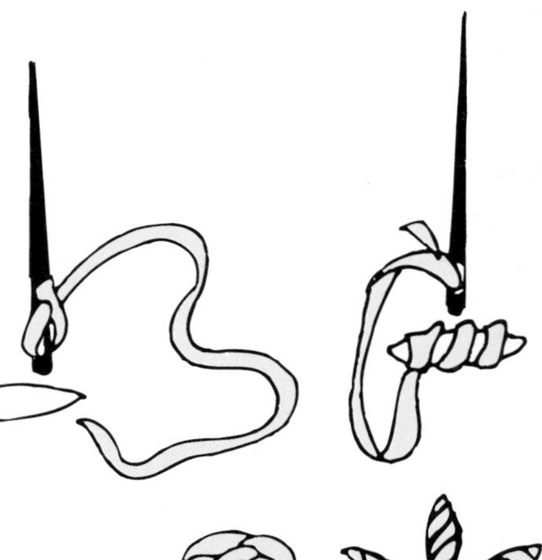

COLONIAL KNOT AND STEM STICH ROSE

Looped 3D Petal Daisies

Make the looped daisies last as they are rather fragile. Cut a 20cm (8") length of ribbon for each daisy. Do not remove the pins until the base of each petal is secured with a colonial knot (or french knot) in two strands of yellow embroidery floss. The centre can be embellished with extra french knots or stamens in extended french knots.

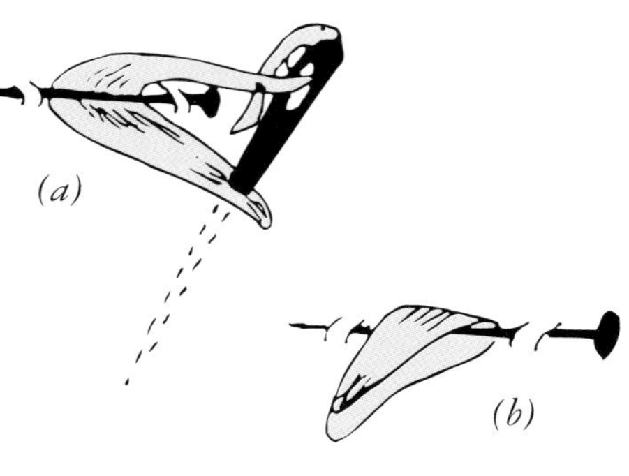

(c)

(d)

Woven Spider's Web Rose

Make five foundation spokes in two strands of matching embroidery floss. Then use the silk ribbon and weave over and under each spoke, starting in the centre and working outwards, controlling the tension as you proceed. Once the spokes are covered and the rose is the required size, take the ribbon through to the back and end off with a backstitch in the foundation fabric.

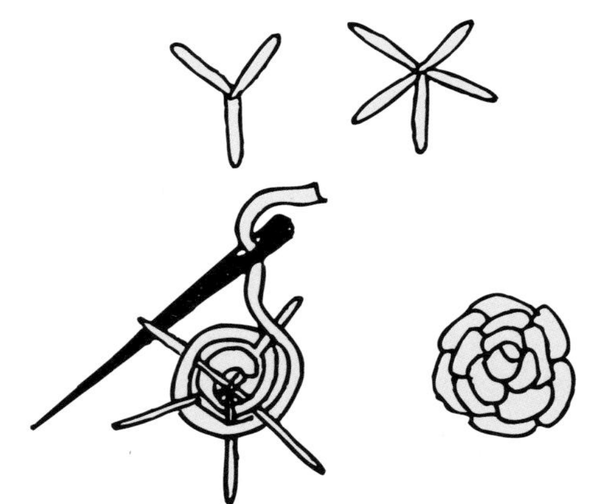

Colonial knot and Lazy Daisy Rosebuds

The rosebud is a combination of a colonial knot surrounded by a lazy daisy.

Bullion-lazy Daisy

Make a single chain stitch and before anchoring it, twist the ribbon twice around the tip of the needle. Pull the needle through the ribbon and anchor into the background.

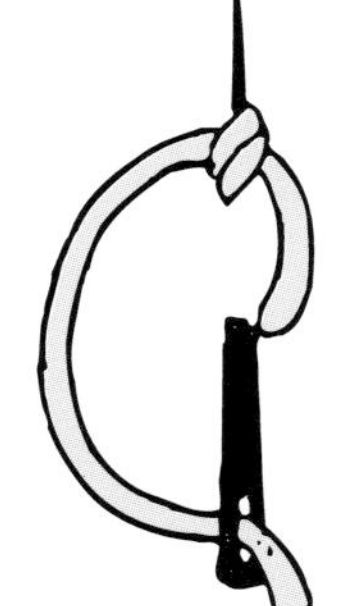

Basket Weave

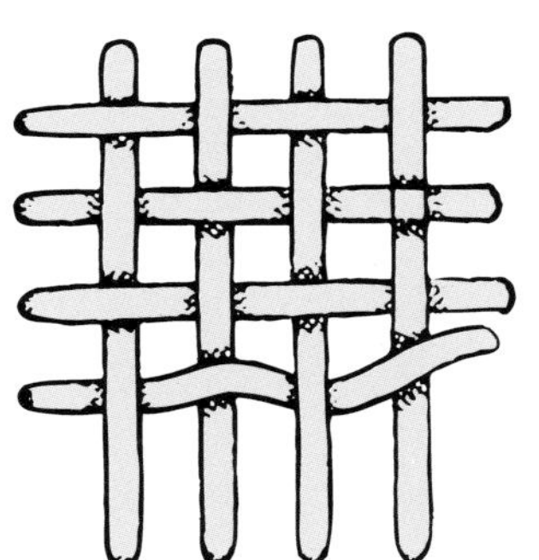

How to Make Fuchsias and Fluted Petals

(Fuchsias, hibiscus, carnation and marigolds)
Bring the silk ribbon through the background fabric. Use a crewel needle with one strand of matching floss and run a gathering thread along one side of the ribbon. Pull up the gathers to create the fluted petals. End the gathering thread securely and pierce the background fabric with the silk ribbon, forming a gathered frill. End each frill with a backstitch on the wrong side of the work.

Basic Fuchsia

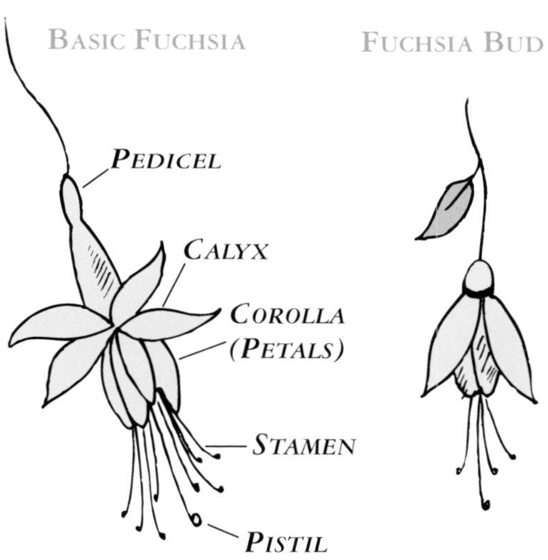

Fuchsia Bud

Fuchsia with a Double Whorl of Petals

Fluted Petals

Drawn up in a circle. Ideal for marigolds, carnations, zinneas and hibiscus

Fluted/ruched Petals

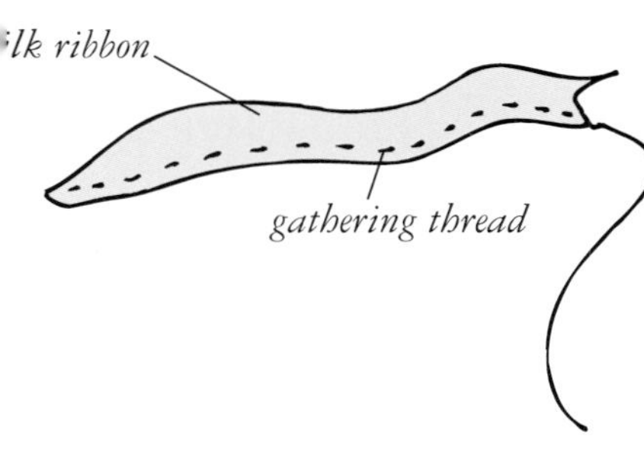

Ideal for a double whorl of petals

Fuchsia Bud Construction

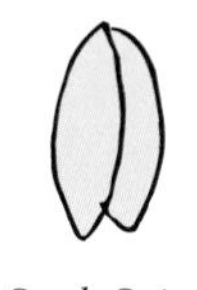

Stab Stitch

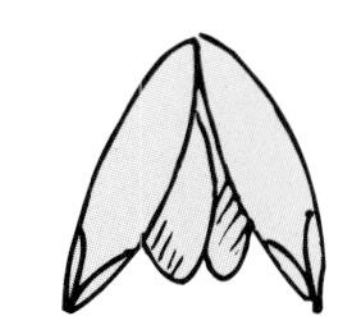

Inverted Stab stitch

Calyx created by pulling a matching floss thread around the top of the inverted stab stitch

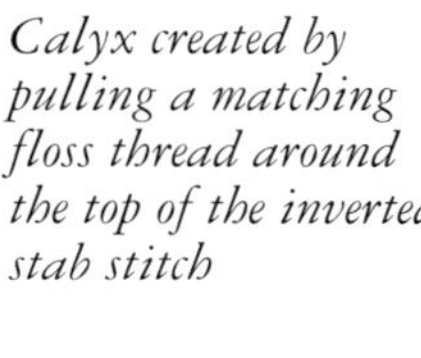

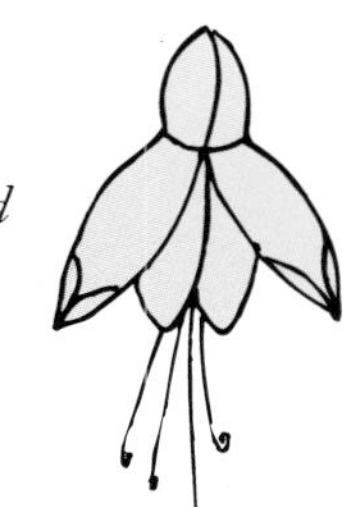

Fluted/gathered Frills

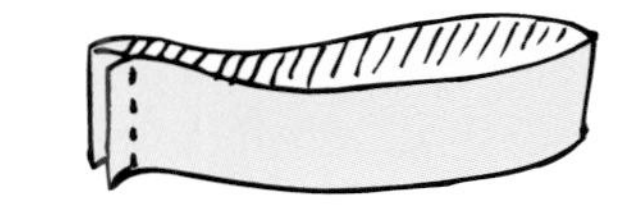

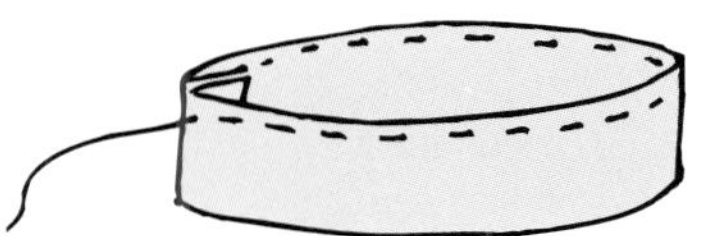

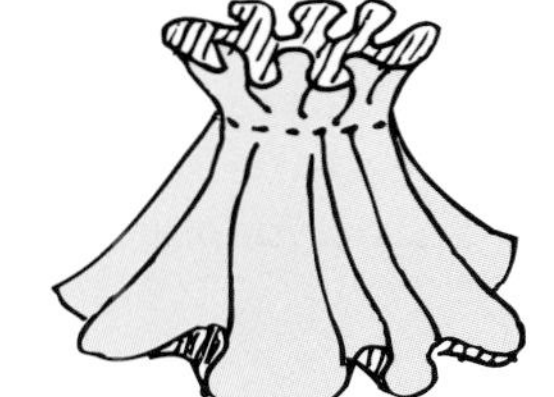

Ideal for larger fuchsias in 7mm wide silk ribbon

Working with Satin Ribbon

These methods can be used for all ribbon types eg. velvet, rayon and taffeta ribbon.

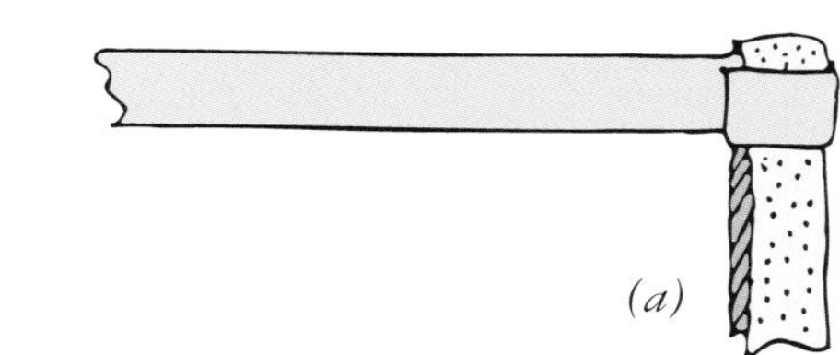
(a)

How to Make Different Satin Ribbon Roses

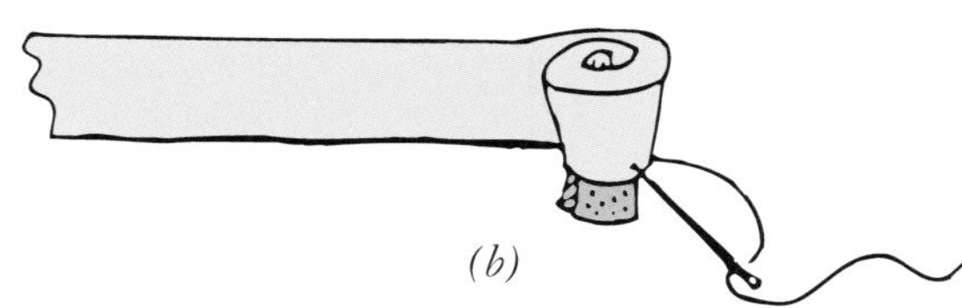
(b)

The Cabbage Rose (or Tab Method)

(Using approximately 8–10mm ($^3/_8$–$^1/_2$") wide satin ribbon)
Cut a short length of ribbon approx 6 cm (2") This is the tab. Fold the tab over the end of the ribbon length, forming a square with the ribbon **(a)**.

Form the bud centre of the rose by rolling the ribbon tightly on itself, a few times, to make a tight tube. Make a couple of small stitches at the base to hold it firm **(b)**.

To form the petals, fold the ribbon backwards so that it is parallel to the tube, forming a 45 degree angle. Roll the tube across the fold, loosely at the top and tightly at the base. Stitch in place with a couple of stitches **(c)**.

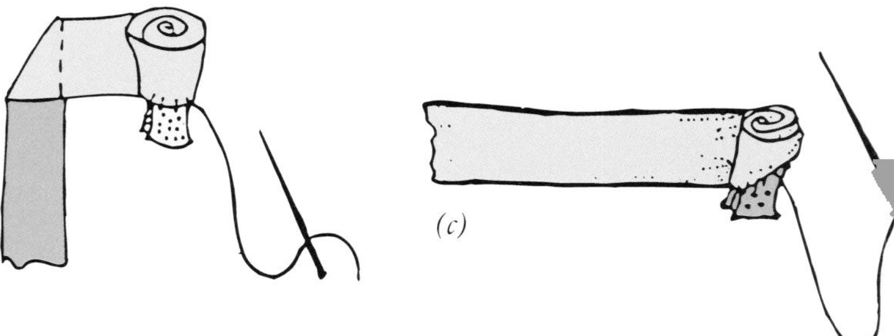

(c)

Continue to fold, roll and stitch, shaping the rose as you work, until it is the desired size. Cut and sear the ribbon by quickly passing it under the base of a candle flame or lighter.

Turn the end under the rose simulating a petal and slip-hem in place. (Cut off the excess tab and sear the base of the rose)
Once you have made a selection of roses, position them onto your background fabric and stitch them in place with tiny, invisible stitches.

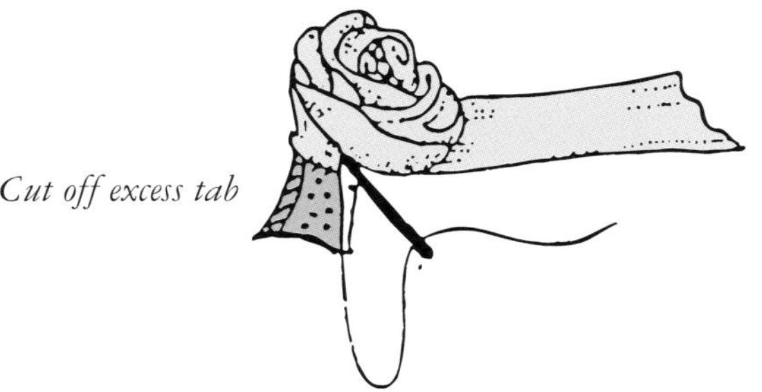

ARGE FLAMBOYANT ROSES

o create these extravagant roses use wide ribbon approx 2-3cm (1") in three ifferent shades – the darker ribbons for the centre of the flower and the paler ibbons for the outer petals. The centre of the rose is made using the tab nethod (see page 70)

he rest of the petals are made separately using a trapezoid shape.

ut three lengths of medium coloured ribbon, 8cm (3") on the long side and five engths of the paler ribbon approximately 8cm (3") on the long side.

ear the diagonal sides under a flame to prevent ravelling. Gather each piece of ibbon with small running stitches. See illustration (a). Stitch the first three etals around the centre of the rose, slightly overlapping each petal. Complete he rose by stitching the five pale petals around the centre shape, again slightly verlapping each petal. Stitch the completed rose onto the background fabric, hecking that all the stitches are hidden. The rose must be good looking from ll angles.

nce you have mastered this rose, enjoy it's potential and play with different ibbon widths and number of petals.

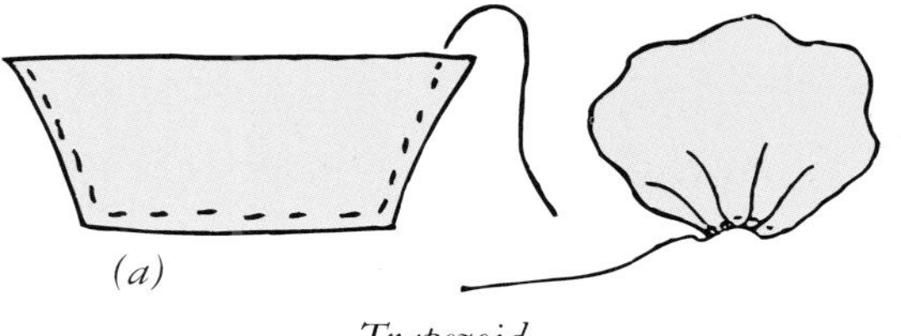

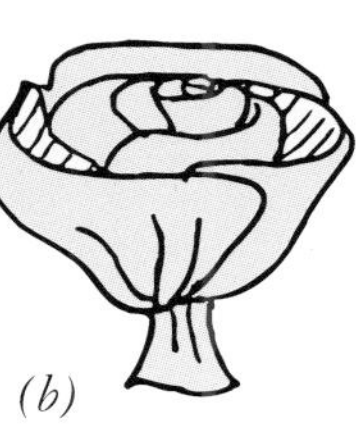

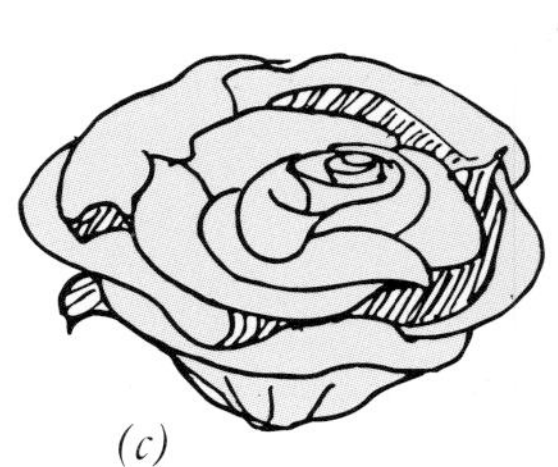

ATIN RIBBON LEAVES

Jsing ribbons approximately 1.5cm ($^{5}/_{8}$") wide, cut a rectangle of ribbon approx cm ($3^{1}/_{4}$") in length. Sear the raw ends by passing the ribbon through the base of flame.

old the top corners to the centre to form a mitred triangle. See sketch **(a)**

un a gathering thread along the seared edges. Pull the gathers up firmly to orm the leaf shape See sketch **(b)**.

uck this edge under the rose and stitch it firmly to the background Sketch **(c)**.

or a stronger leaf, use a double thread brought through the tip of the leaf and ecure it into the background.

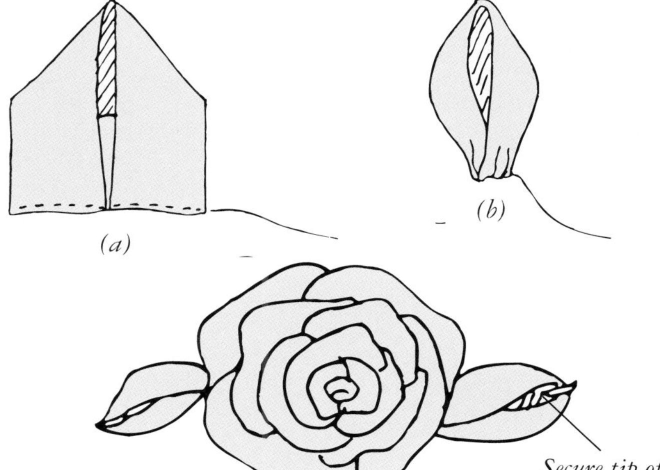

Large Rosebud with Calyx

Use the tab method (see page 70) to create the rosebud, ribbon approx 2cm (3/4") wide. Make the leaf shape as described on page 71, and tuck the tab method rosebud into the calyx shape. Manipulate the petals and the calyx into an attractive shape as you attach it to the background.

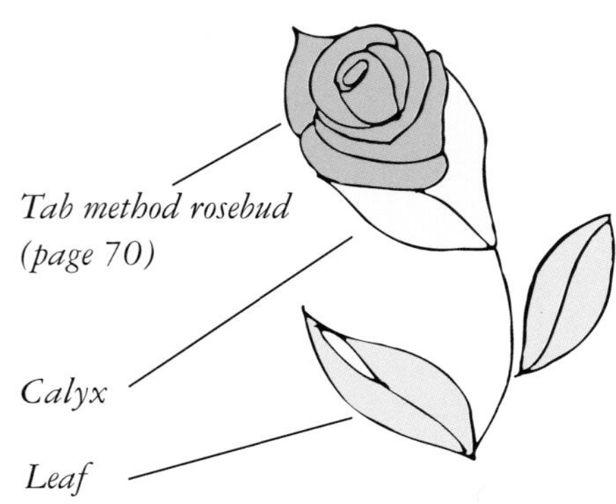

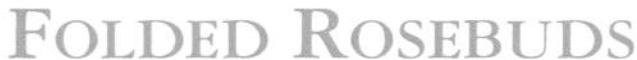

Folded Rosebuds

Make folded rosebuds from a rectangle of ribbon approx 2cm x 7.5cm (3/4" x 3")

1. Fold the left side down at right angles to the centre.
2. Fold the right side down so that it runs parallel to the diagonal left side, leaving a small space 6mm (1/4").
3. Fold the left side from the left to the right at an angle, about 25mm (1") from the point.
4. Fold the right hand side, from right to left at an angle, about 25mm (1") from the point and secure the cross-over with a pin or a stitch. Trim the base of the folded rose to fit neatly into the calyx.
5. Pin the folded edges in place and applique the calyx to the rosebud. Hem the outer edge of the rose to the background but leave the inner fold of the bud free.

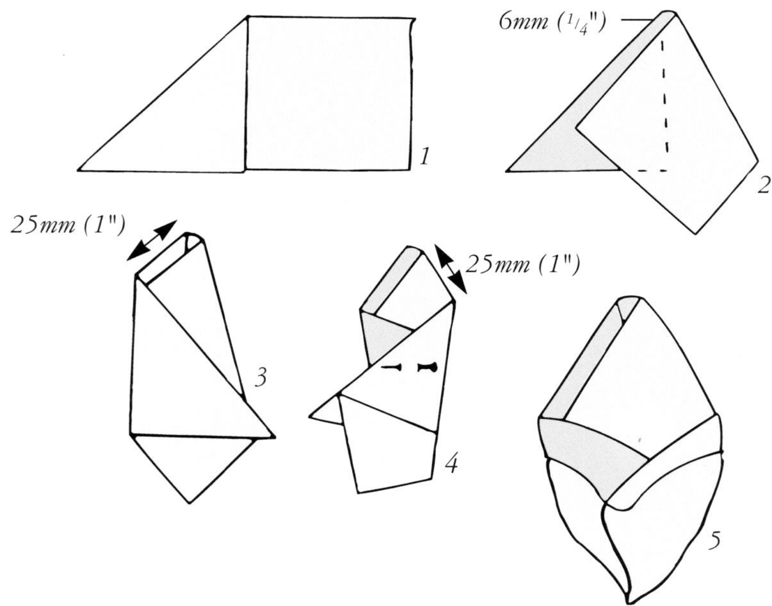

Crewel Stitch Glossary

A Note to Left-handed Embroiders:
Look at the stitch in a mirror or make a photocopy of the stitch, hold the paper up to the light on the reverse side and sketch your own left-handed stitch.

Outline Stitches and Border Stitches

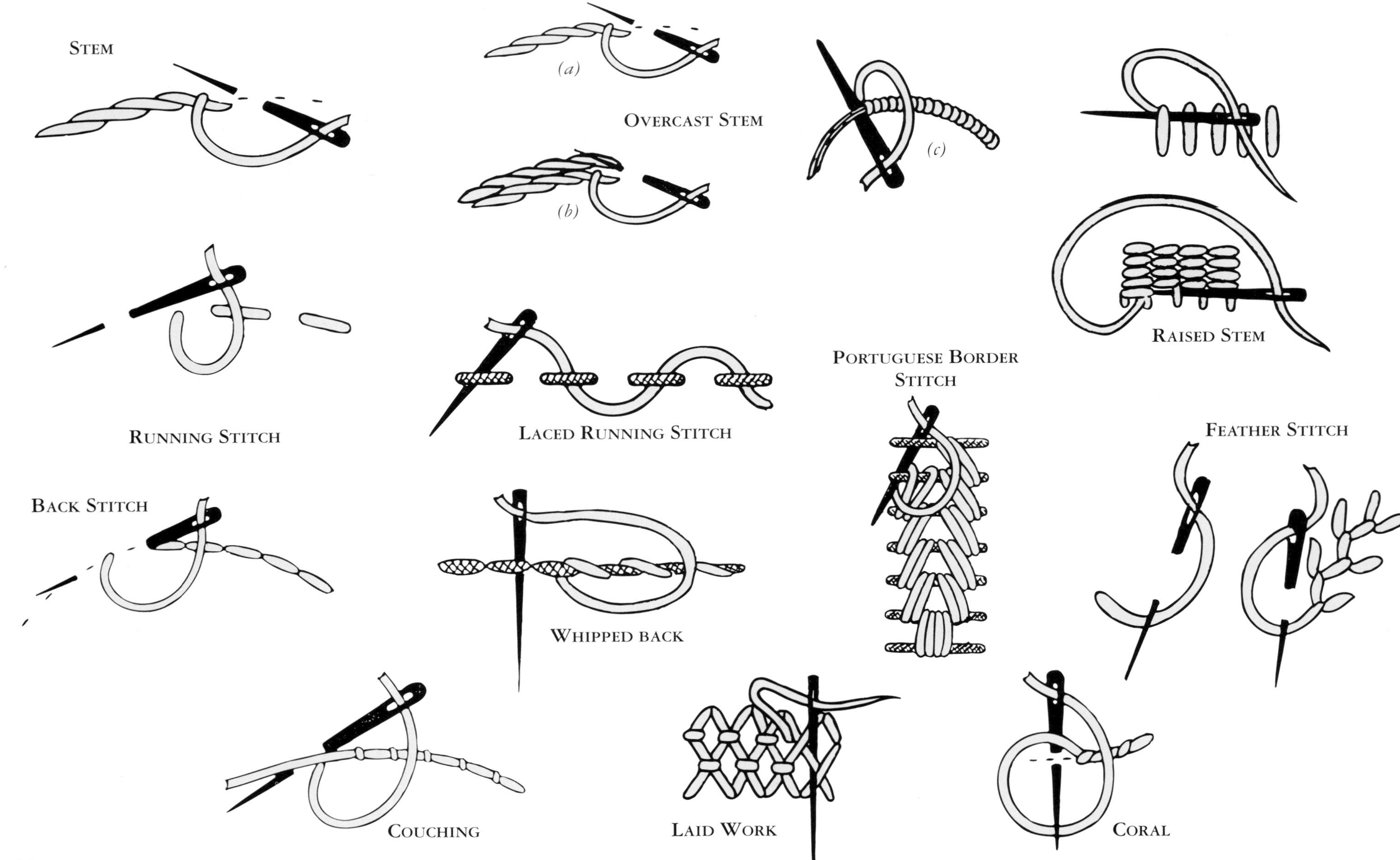

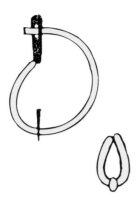

CHAIN

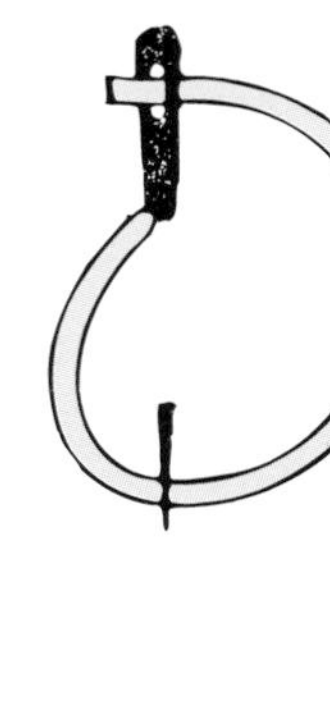

DETACHED CHAIN (LAZY DAISY)

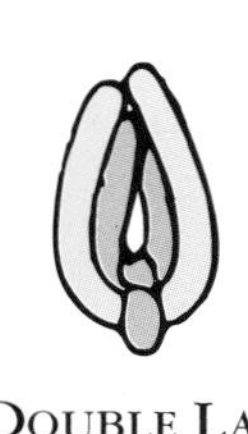

DOUBLE LAZY DAISY

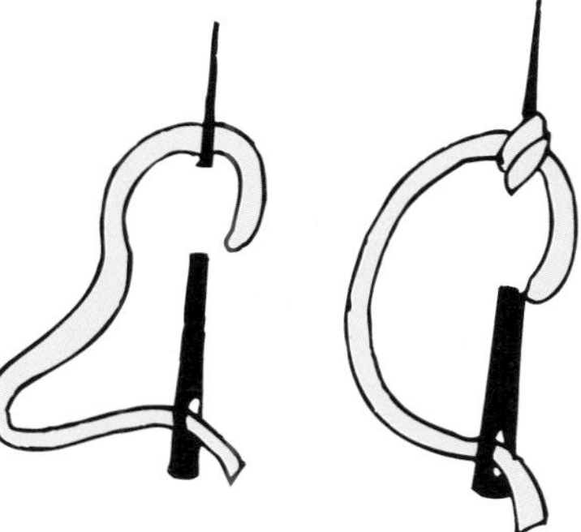

BULLION-LAZY DAISY COMBINATION

WHIPPED CHAIN

RAISED CHAIN

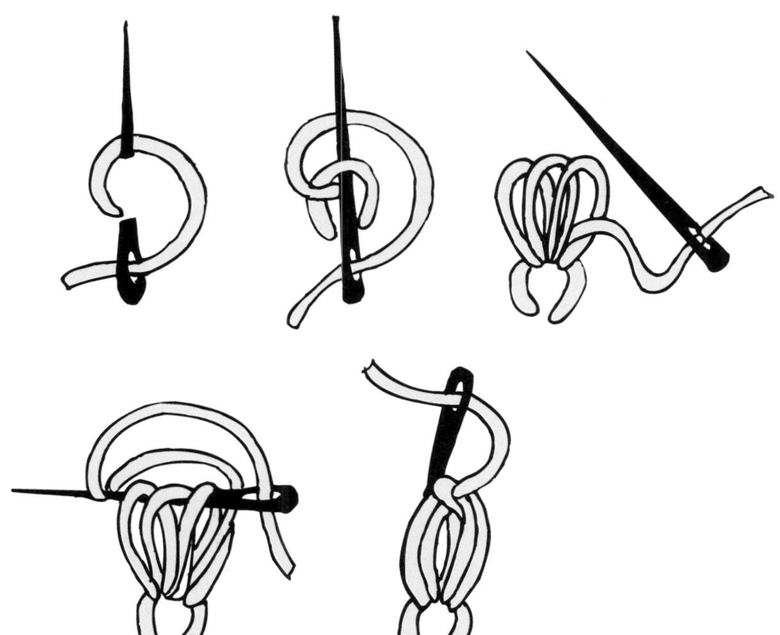

NUT STITCH

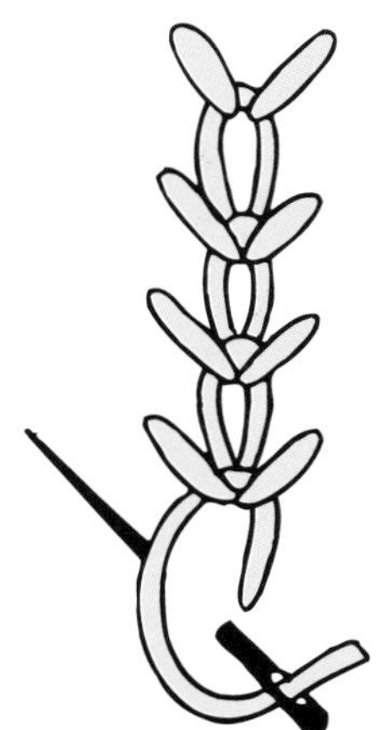

WHEATEAR

Buttonhole Stitches

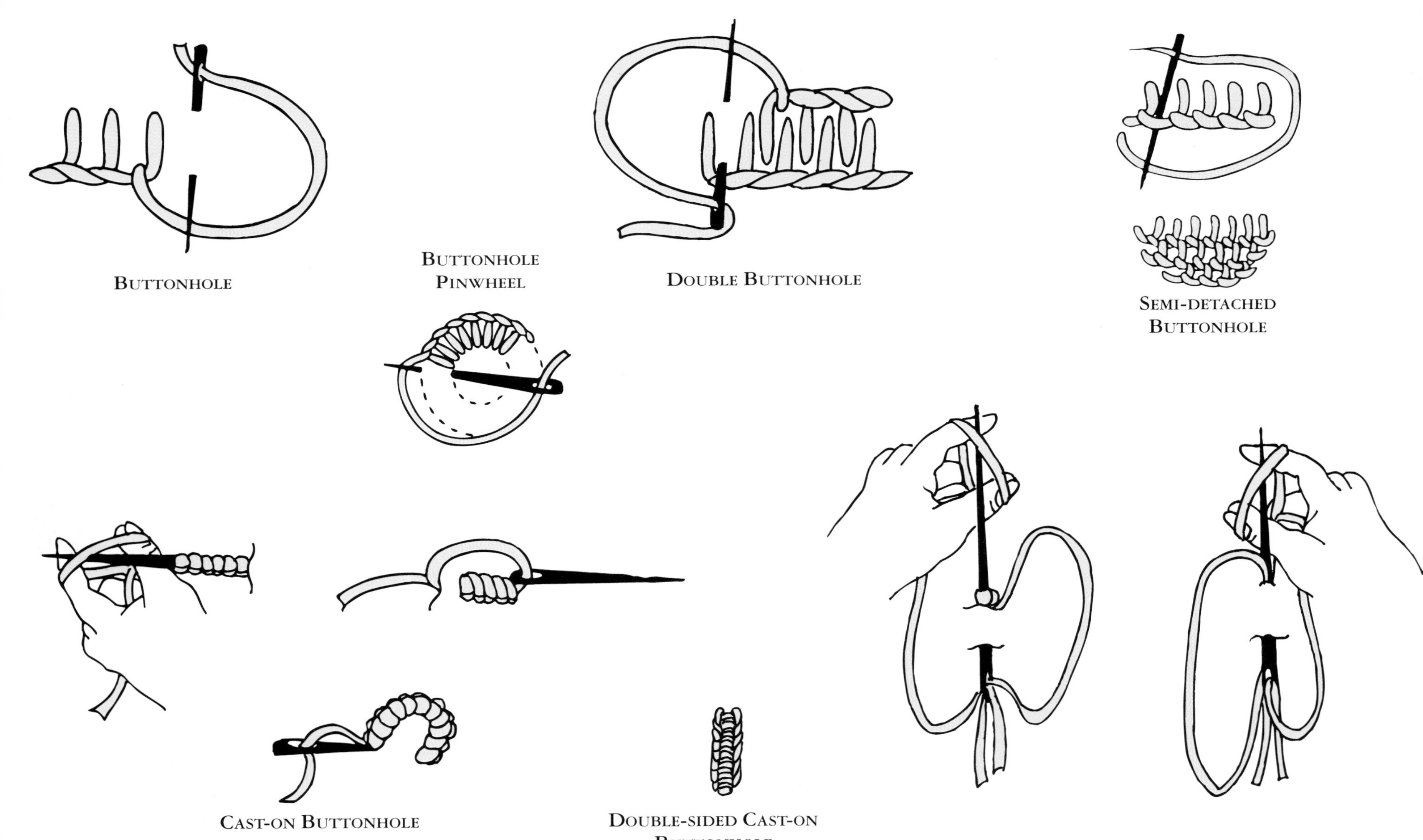

Buttonhole

Buttonhole Pinwheel

Double Buttonhole

Semi-detached Buttonhole

Cast-on Buttonhole

Double-sided Cast-on Buttonhole

Isolated and Filling Stitches

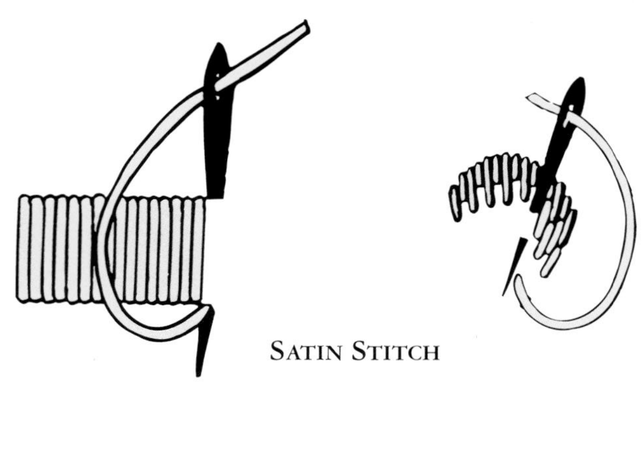

Satin Stitch

Straight or Stab Stitch

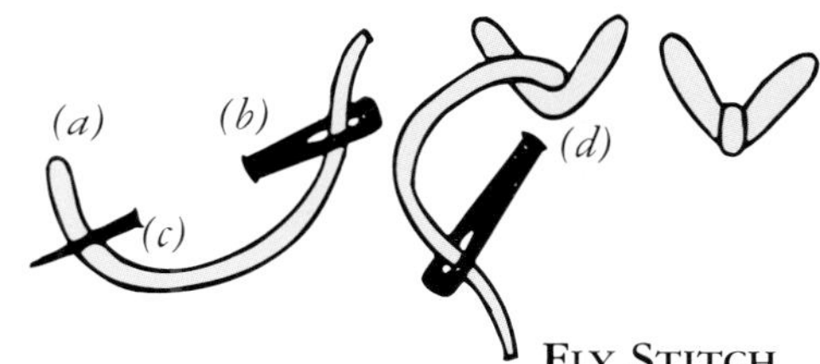

Fly Stitch

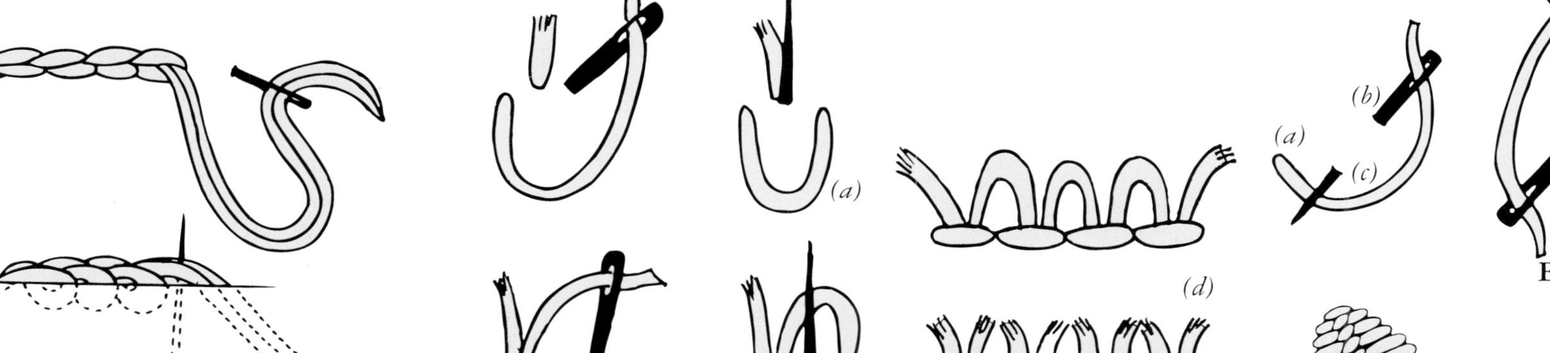

Split Stitch

Extended Fly Stitch

Tufting
(Turkey Work)

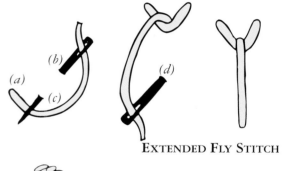

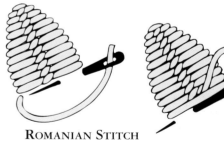

Romanian Stitch

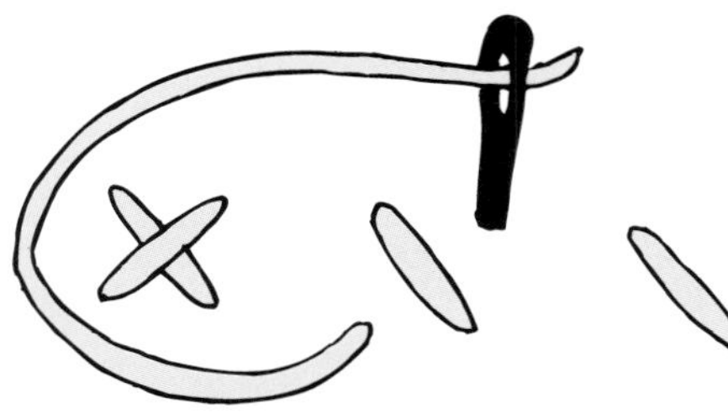

Cross Stitch

Cretan Stitch

Fishbone Stitch

Woven Stitches

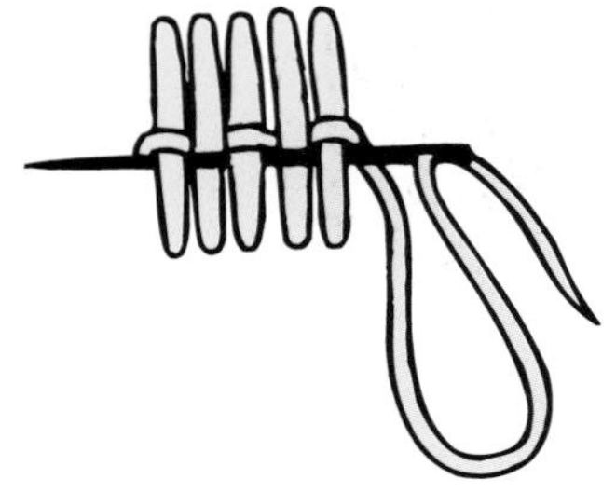

Weaving

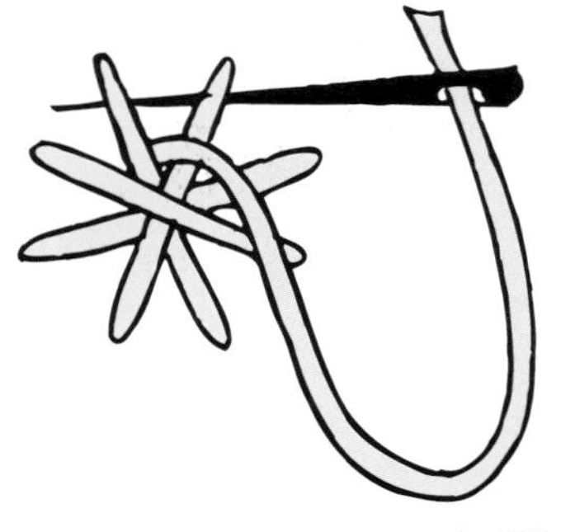

Whipped Spider's Web

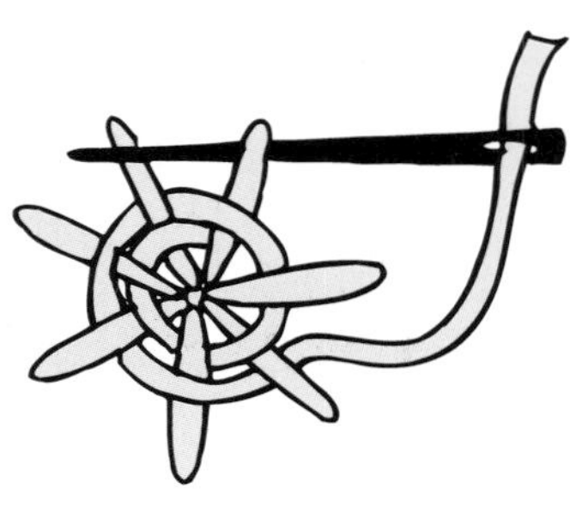

Woven Spider's Web

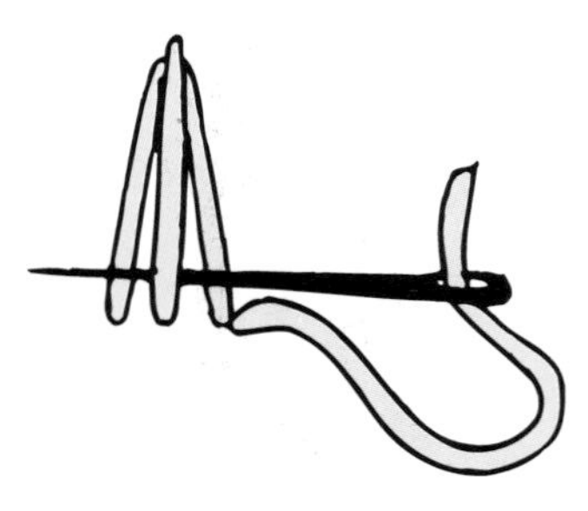

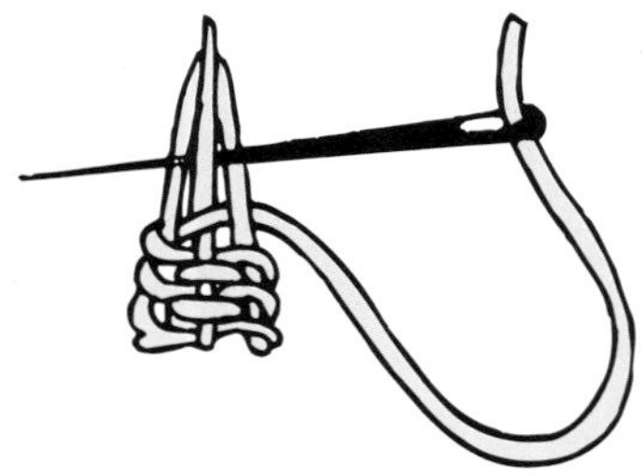

Woven Picot

Pekinese

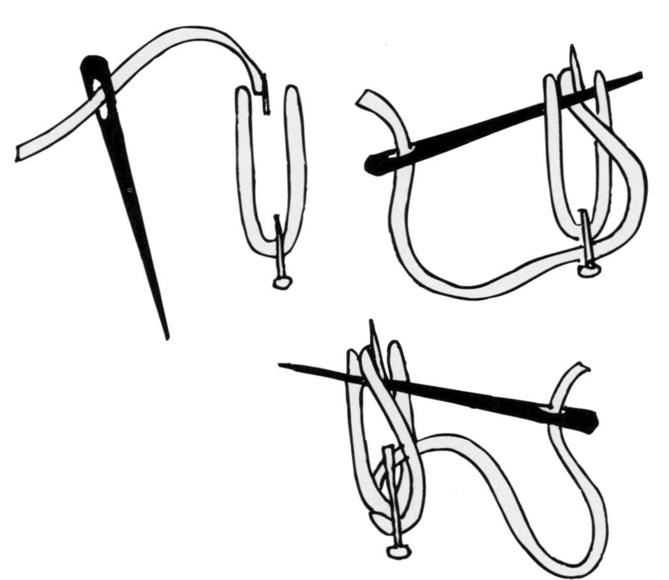

Detached Woven Picot

Bullion Rosebud

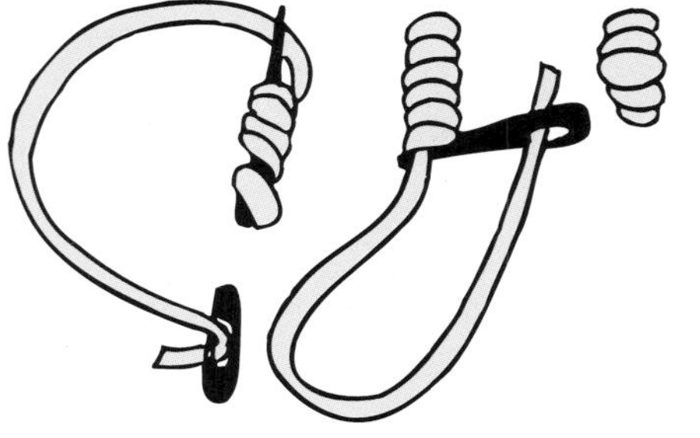

Basic Bullion Knot

Grub Rose

Looped Bullion

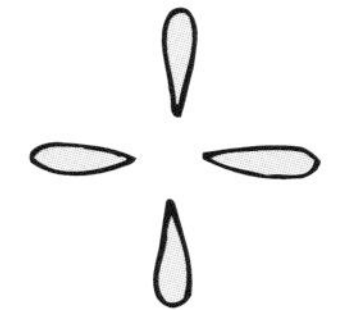

Bullion Daisy

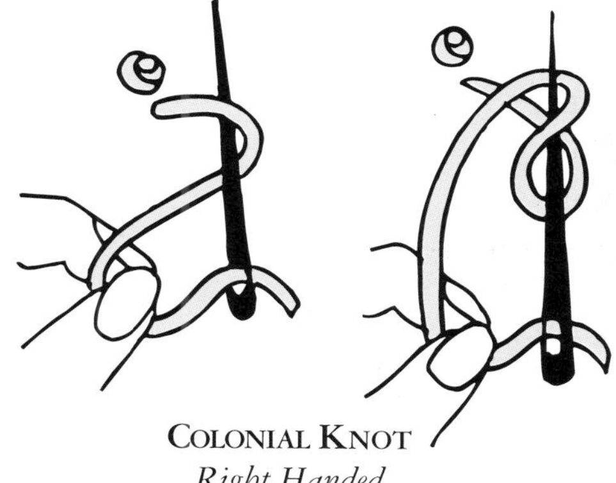

Colonial Knot
Right Handed

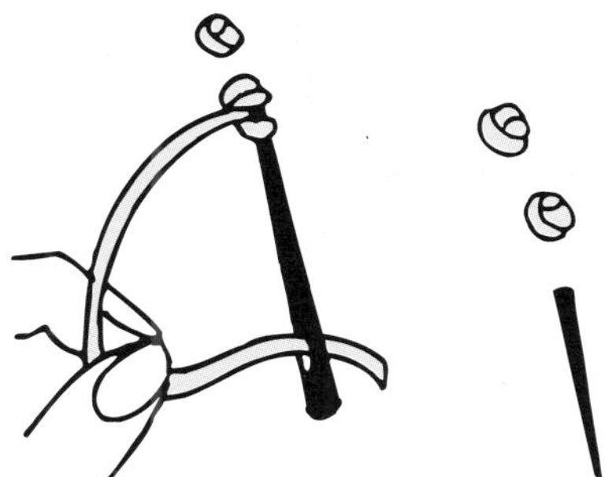

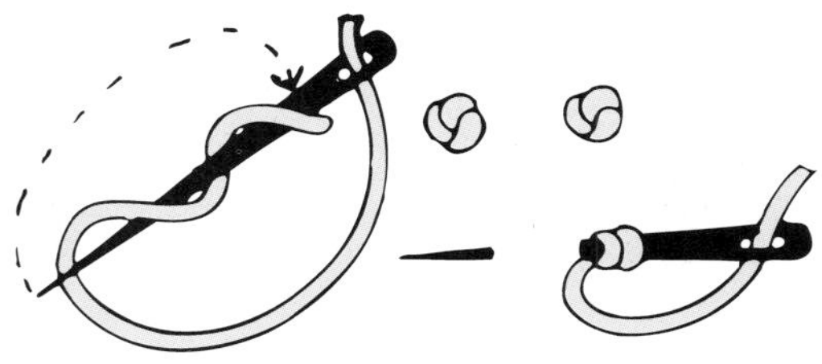

French Knot

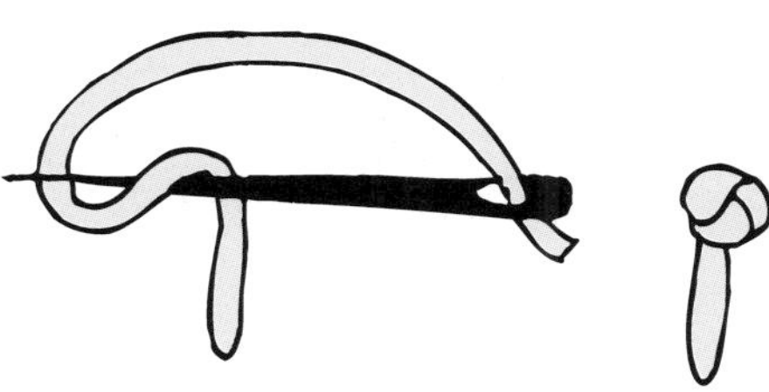

Extended French Knot

A Floral ABC

A Floral ABC

Sweet Sixteen Sampler

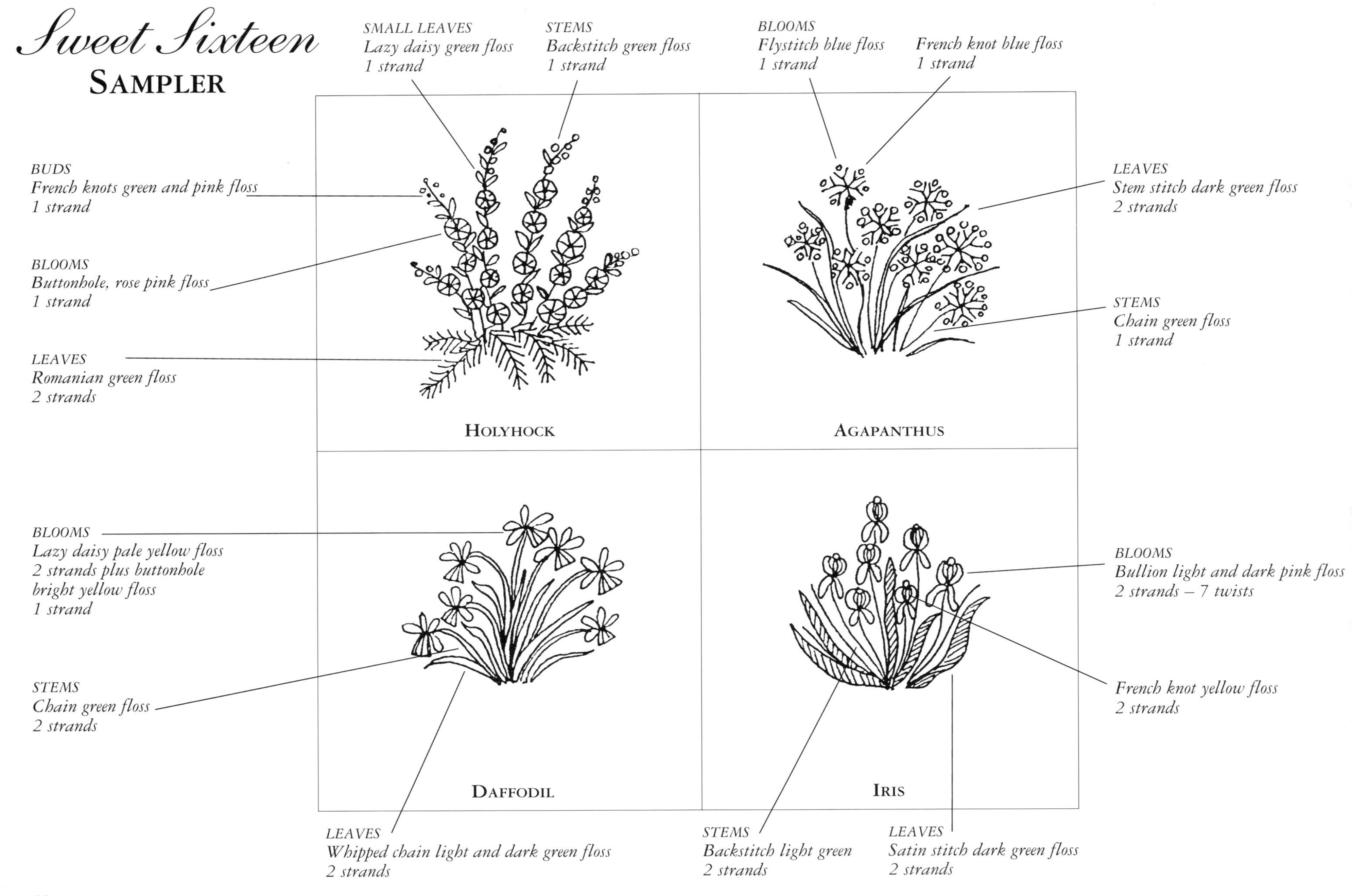

Sweet Sixteen
SAMPLER

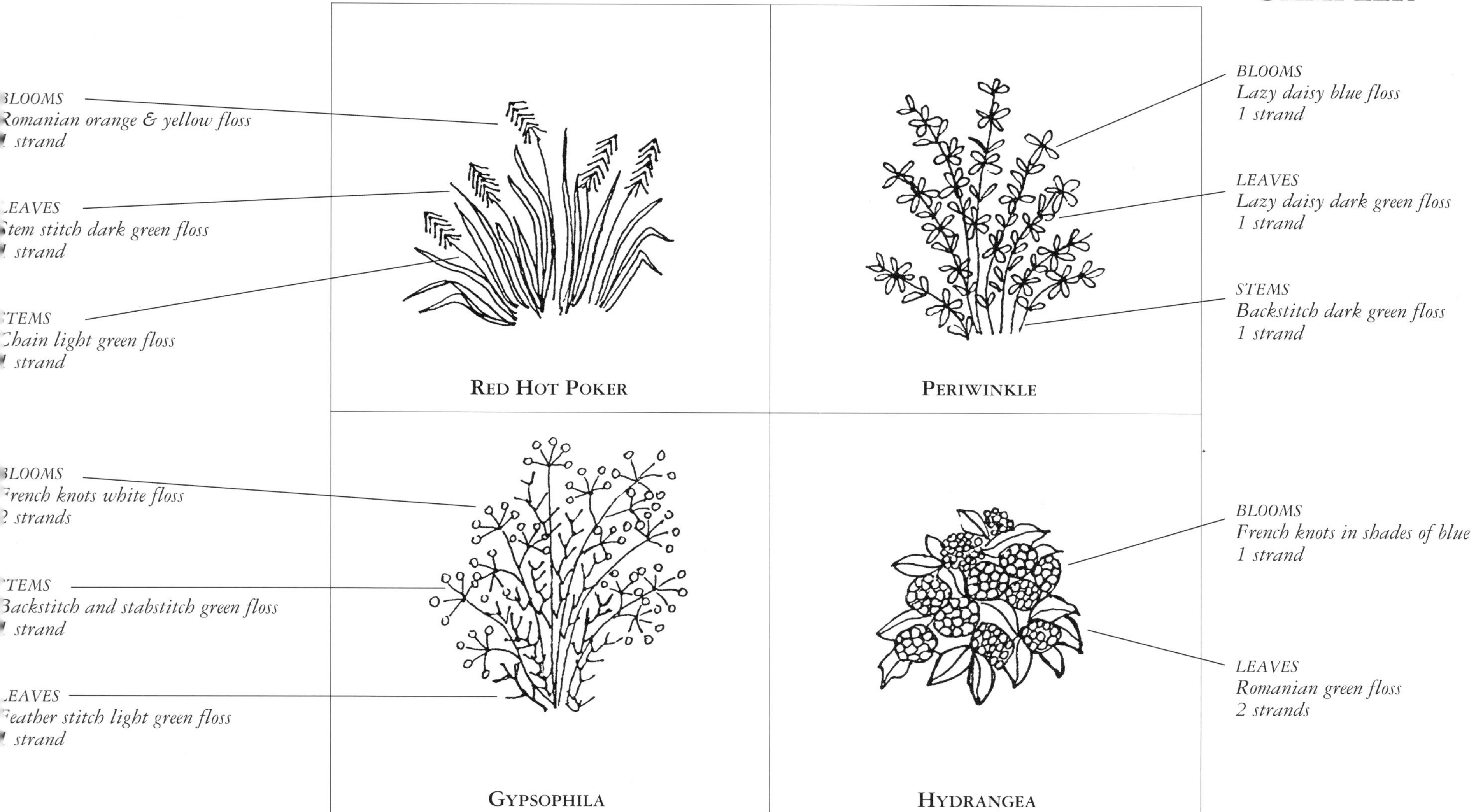

BORDER Whipped chain ecru floss 2 strands, light green 2 strands

Sweet Sixteen Sampler

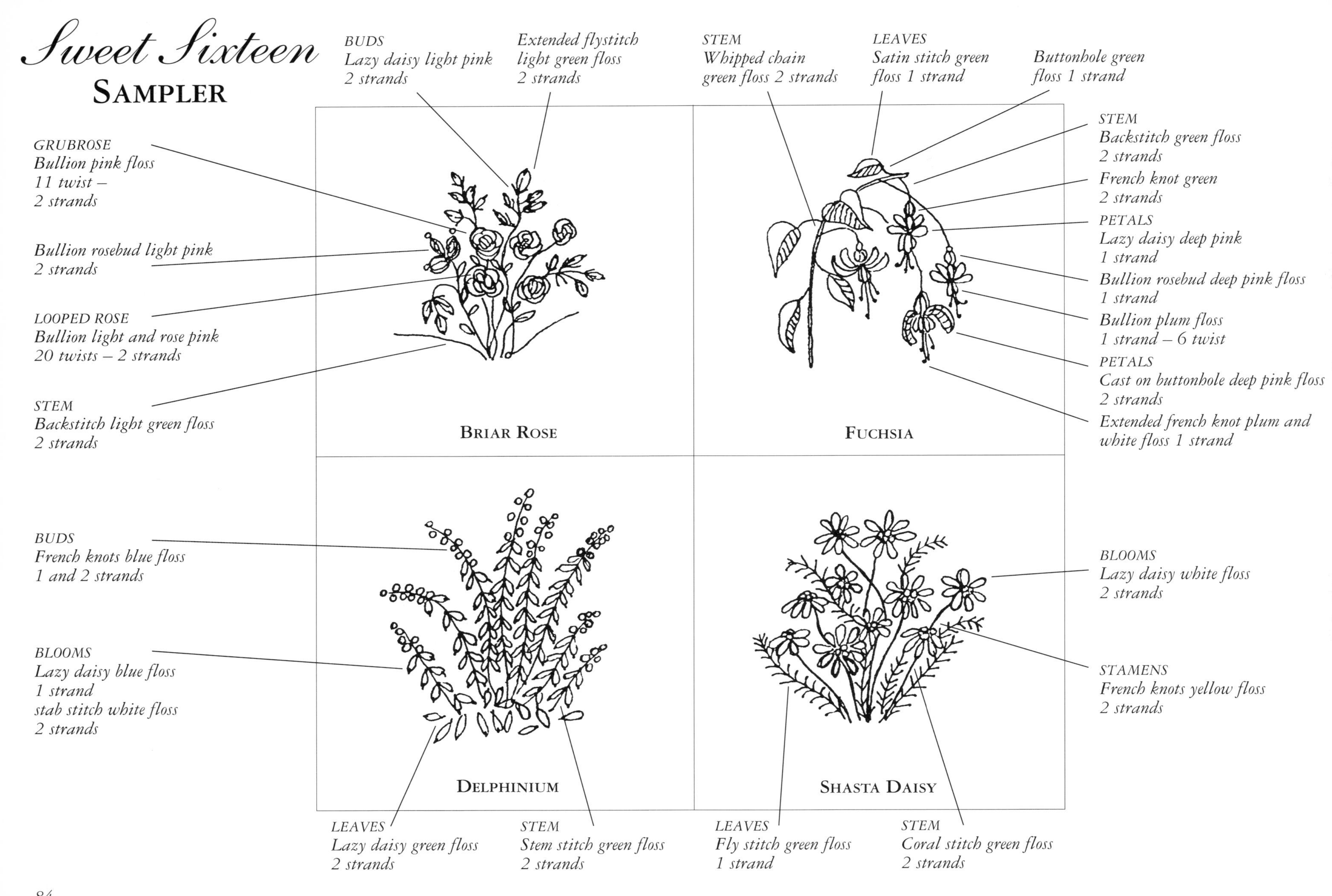

BUDS
*Lazy daisy light pink
2 strands*

*Extended flystitch
light green floss
2 strands*

STEM
*Whipped chain
green floss 2 strands*

LEAVES
*Satin stitch green
floss 1 strand*

*Buttonhole green
floss 1 strand*

STEM
*Backstitch green floss
2 strands*

*French knot green
2 strands*

PETALS
*Lazy daisy deep pink
1 strand*

*Bullion rosebud deep pink floss
1 strand*

*Bullion plum floss
1 strand – 6 twist*

PETALS
*Cast on buttonhole deep pink floss
2 strands*

*Extended french knot plum and
white floss 1 strand*

GRUBROSE
*Bullion pink floss
11 twist –
2 strands*

*Bullion rosebud light pink
2 strands*

LOOPED ROSE
*Bullion light and rose pink
20 twists – 2 strands*

STEM
*Backstitch light green floss
2 strands*

BRIAR ROSE

FUCHSIA

BUDS
*French knots blue floss
1 and 2 strands*

BLOOMS
*Lazy daisy blue floss
1 strand
stab stitch white floss
2 strands*

BLOOMS
*Lazy daisy white floss
2 strands*

STAMENS
*French knots yellow floss
2 strands*

DELPHINIUM

SHASTA DAISY

LEAVES
*Lazy daisy green floss
2 strands*

STEM
*Stem stitch green floss
2 strands*

LEAVES
*Fly stitch green floss
1 strand*

STEM
*Coral stitch green floss
2 strands*

84

Sweet Sixteen Sampler

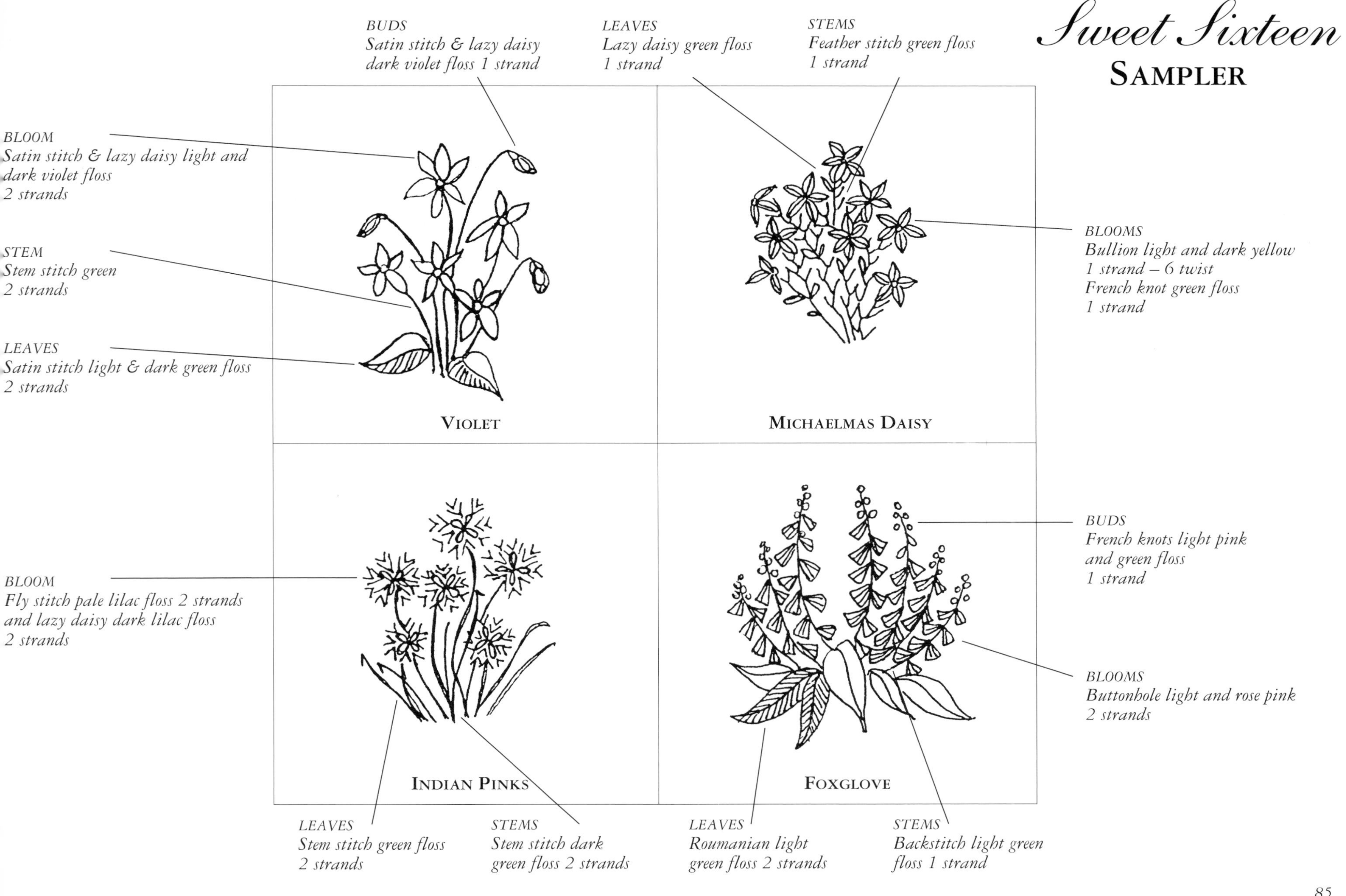

Victoriana

A Signature Pillow (Hannah)

Raised stem blue floss
1 strand
Double-sided
cast-on buttonhole
mustard
silk thread
2 strands
Bullion green floss (1 strand)
Overast stem green floss 2 strands
Raised stem pink silk thread
1 strand
Grub rose pink floss
2 strands
Extended French
knots pink floss
2 strands
Romanian green floss
2 strands
Colonial knots white
no. 8 candlewick threa
STEMS
Whipped backstitch
green floss
2 strands
Buttonhole daisy
pink floss
1 strand
Extended French kno
pink floss
1 strand
Bullion-lazy daisy
combination pink
silk thread
1 strand
Fly stitch white and
green floss
2 strands
French knot forget-me-not
blue and yellow floss
2 strands
LEAVES
Bullion knot green floss
1 strand
GYPSOPHILA
Colonial knot and fly
stitch white and green floss
2 strands
Bullion daisy yellow floss
1 strand

Victoriana
Antique Embroidered Pin Cushion/ Lavender Bag

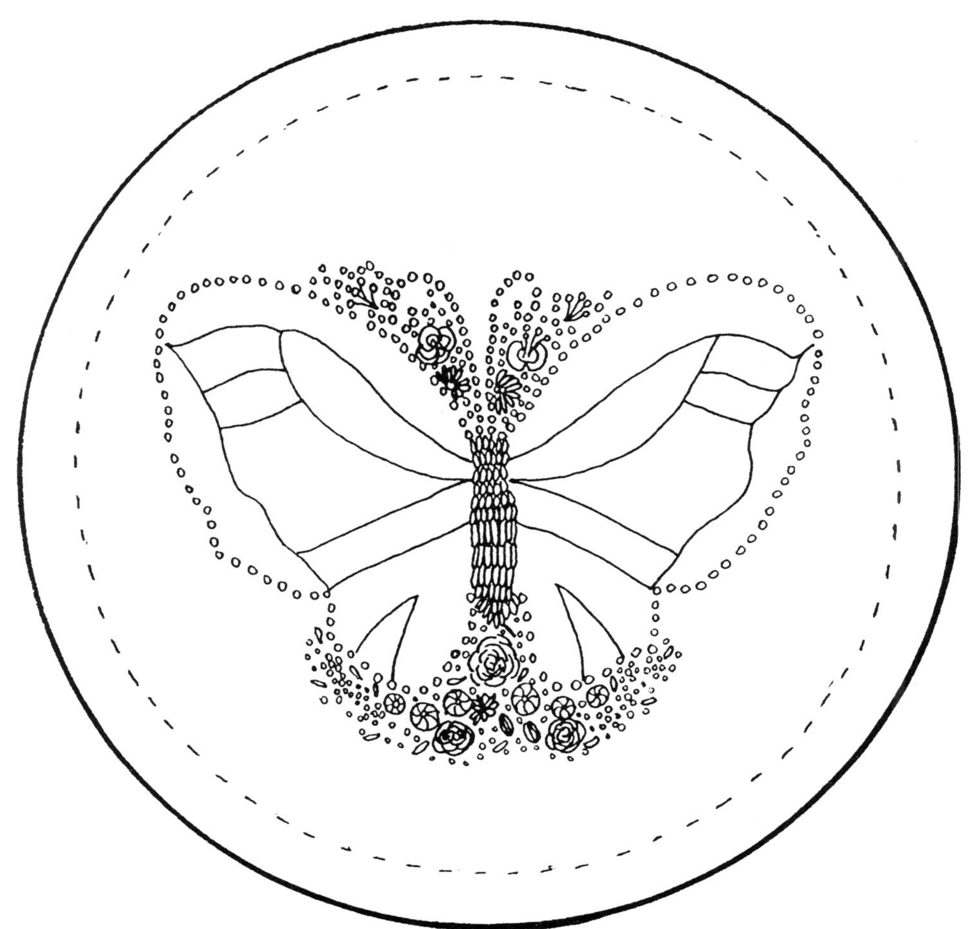

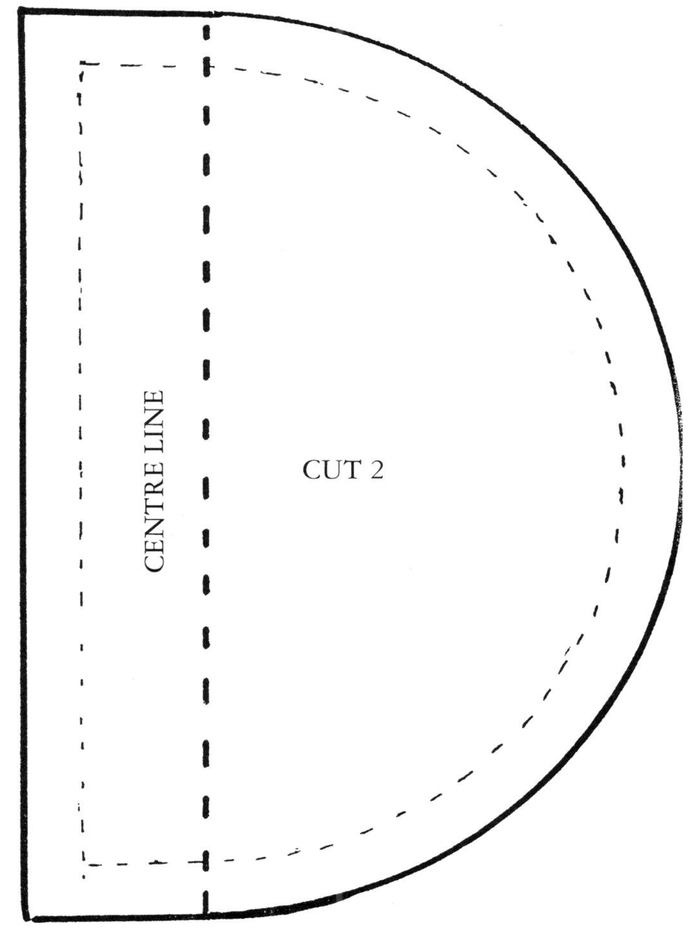

Enlarge this pattern by 125%
for the designs on p.30 & p31.

Fragile Fynbos
QUINTET

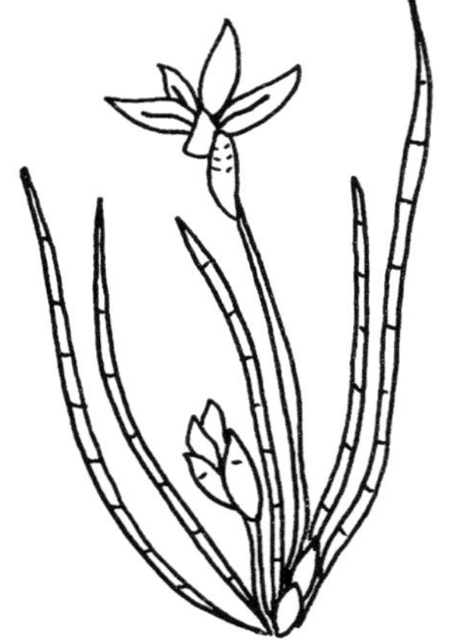

Creepers and Crawlies

BUTTERFLIES IN FULL FLIGHT

Creepers and Crawlies

Daisies and Forget-me-nots Intertwined

Herb Garden
A Minature Herb Sampler

Two strands unless otherwise stated

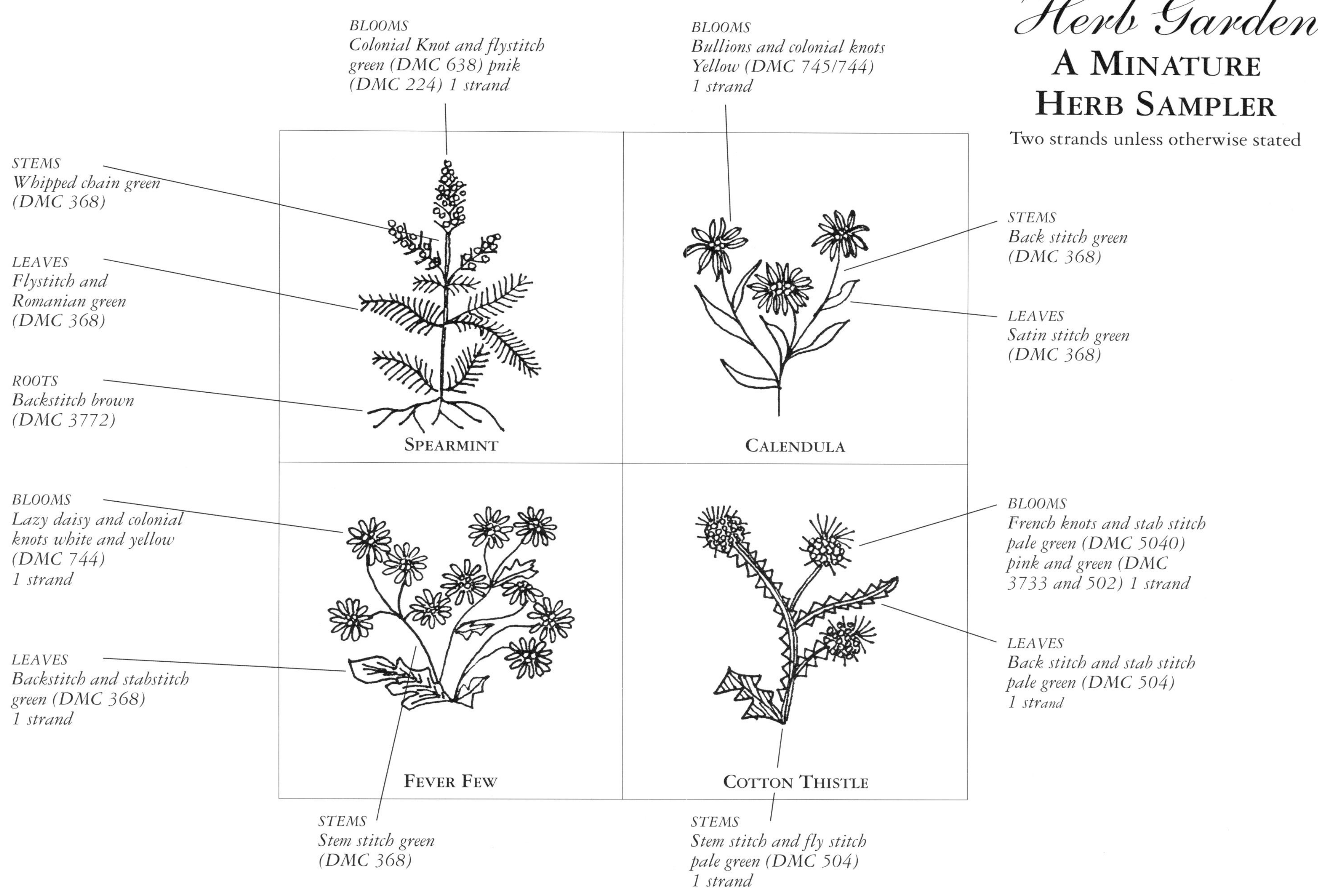

BLOOMS
Colonial Knot and flystitch green (DMC 638) pnik (DMC 224) 1 strand
BLOOMS
Bullions and colonial knots Yellow (DMC 745/744) 1 strand
STEMS
Whipped chain green (DMC 368)
LEAVES
Flystitch and Romanian green (DMC 368)
ROOTS
Backstitch brown (DMC 3772)
SPEARMINT
STEMS
Back stitch green (DMC 368)
LEAVES
Satin stitch green (DMC 368)
CALENDULA
BLOOMS
Lazy daisy and colonial knots white and yellow (DMC 744) 1 strand
LEAVES
Backstitch and stabstitch green (DMC 368) 1 strand
FEVER FEW
BLOOMS
French knots and stab stitch pale green (DMC 5040) pink and green (DMC 3733 and 502) 1 strand
LEAVES
Back stitch and stab stitch pale green (DMC 504) 1 strand
COTTON THISTLE
STEMS
Stem stitch green (DMC 368)
STEMS
Stem stitch and fly stitch pale green (DMC 504) 1 strand

Herb Garden

A Minature Herb Sampler

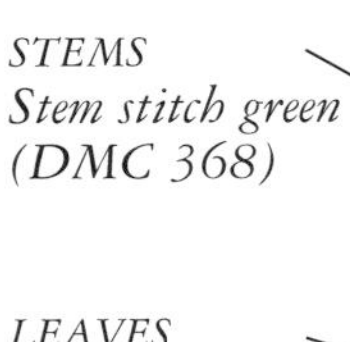

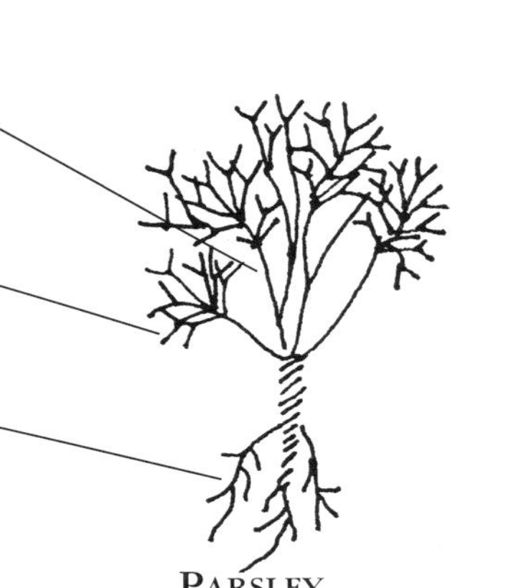

BLOOMS Bullion lilac and purple (DMC 869 and 871)

STEMS Stem stitch pale green (DMC 504)

LEAVES Bullion green (DMC 502)

ROOTS Backstitch and chain brown (DMC 452)

BLOOMS
Bullion pinks (DMC 223 and 224) and extended french knots yellow, white and beige (DMC 745 and 950)

STEMS
Stem stitch green (DMC 368)

LEAVES
Fly stitch green (DMC 501 & 368)

ROOTS
Satin and backstitch mustard green (DMC 372) 1 strand

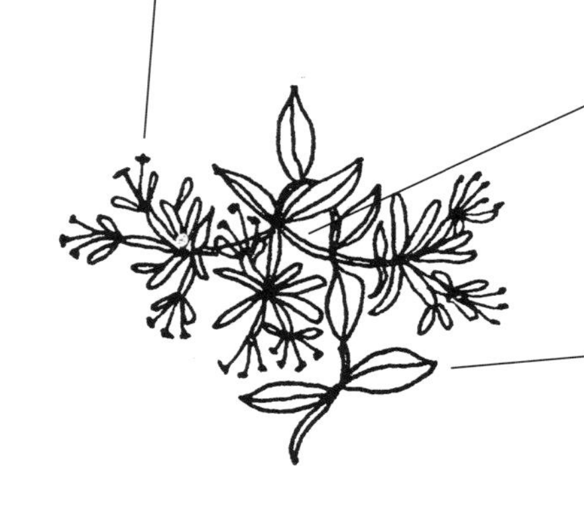

STEMS
Whipped chain brown and green (DMC 840 and 368)

LEAVES
Fishbone green (DMC 368) 1 strand

PARSLEY

LAVENDER

HONEYSUCKLE

BLOOMS
Stab stitch and colonial knots yellow and green (DMC 744 & 3046 & 503)

BUD
Lazy daisy yellow and green (DMC 744 & 501) 1 strand

LEAVES
Fishbone green (DMC 501)

STEMS
Overcast stem green (DMC 501)

LEAVES
Buttonhole dark green (DMC 500) 1 strand

STEMS
Whipped backstitch light and dark green (DMC 502 and 500)

ROOTS
Backstitch and stab stitch brown (DMC 840)

ARNICA

ROSEMARY

VIOLA

ROOTS
Stab and backstitch brown (DMC 840) 1 strand

BLOOMS Lazy daisy and extended french knots lilac (DMC 3041) 1 strand

LEAVES Bullion green (DMC 502)

STEM Coral stitch brown (DMC 841)

BLOOMS AND BUDS
Stab stitch violet (DMC 208) 1 strand and colonial knot yellow (DMC 744)

Herb Garden

A Minature Herb Sampler

BLOOMS Lazy daisy and french knots lilac, pink and white (DMC 3042 and 224)

STEMS Whipped chain green (DMC 502)

LEAVES Whipped chain green (DMC 502)

TEM
hain dark green
DMC 500)
strand

EAVES
ishbone dark green
DMC 500) and
ackstitch light
reen (DMC 503)

BAY

CHIVES

TARRAGON

BLOOMS
French knots white and green (DMC 502)

STEM
Whipped chain green and brown (DMC 368 and 3772)

LEAVES
Bullion dark green (DMC 501)

LOOMS
tab stitch orange
nd yellow (DMC
77 and 744)
strand

EAVES
uttonhole green
DMC 368)
strand

NASTURTIUM

STEMS
Stem stitch green (DMC 503)

DILL

BLOOMS French knots yellows (DMC 744/7450)

LEAVES Flystitch green (DMC 503)

LARGE STEM Double buttonhole green threaded with white (DMC 502)

STEMS Whipped chain green (DMC 503)

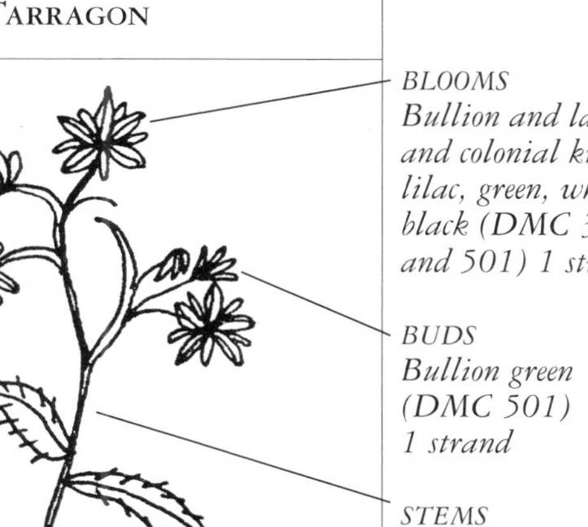

BORAGE

BLOOMS
Bullion and lazy daisy and colonial knot lilac, green, white and black (DMC 3041 and 501) 1 strand

BUDS
Bullion green (DMC 501) 1 strand

STEMS
Chain green (DMC 368)

LEAVES Split stitch green (DMC 502/501) and stab stitch white 1 strand

Enchanted Gardens

Terracotta Terrace at Colenso Road

An Enchanted Garden

Enchanted Gardens

Twin Tubs in a Lighter Shade of Pale